THE CHURCH'S POSITION
ON DANCING

ABBE HENRI LOUIS HULOT

The Church's Position on Dancing was originally published as *Balls and Dancing Parties Condemned by the Scriptures, Holy Fathers, Holy Councils, and Most Renowned Theologians of the Church* by Patrick Donahoe in 1857, and is in the public domain.

ISBN: 978-1-957066-41-7

Mediatrix Press Edition © 2023.

This edition has been updated with editorial changes to correct grammar and punctuation mistakes, rewording for clarity, and minor corrections to typographical errors. Additionally, certain names have been updated to reflect modern usage. Every effort has been made to preserve the original meaning and intent of the author, these changes were made to enhance the readability and accessibility of the text.

mediatrixpress.com

CONTENTS

PREFACE

TO THE AMERICAN EDITION

The following translation of Father Hulot's treatise on Dances is from the *Fourth Paris edition of* 1842 *Traité sur la Danse.* A work of this kind, now introduced for the first time to the English reader, supplies a want felt not only by the pious laity, but, at times, even by the missionary charged with their instruction. The moral dangers of the too common and too fashionable amusements of which it treats are pointed out, with as much force as clearness and learning, in this small but valuable book.

Familiarity removes, often, a due appreciation even of these dangers, and both in cities and country places there are Catholics who seem, as it were, to have become skeptical as to the very existence of the danger attendant on their supposed innocent recreations.

It is but seldom, in these days of error and laxity of morals, that the tastes and habits of what is termed genteel society are regulated upon principles and rules of Christian morality.

With multitudes of worldly people, it is deemed a sufficient guarantee of propriety for any custom or practice whatever, that it prevails, and is in favorable acceptance amongst "the better classes of society," by which they understand, not the virtuous portion of the community, but only that which is rich.

The high and holy testimonies cited in this work, to prove the dangers, and, generally, pernicious consequences of balls and other dancing assemblies, collected as they are with so much care and fidelity, by the learned author, from the saints and holy fathers and councils of the church, render it more particularly valuable in this country, where, owing to the scarcity of Catholic libraries, the learned themselves cannot conveniently have access to the works from which Father Hulot has selected his quotations.

The fidelity of these citations is unquestionable, for even the most unscrupulous writer dare not, and certainly could not with impunity, under the eyes of the doctors of the Sorbonne, and in a city like the French capital, possessing so many libraries, risk even a careless citation, to say nothing of perpetrating a forged extract.

What, then, can the advocates of balls and dances, who are so apt to be offended when their favorite amusements are even mentioned disparagingly, say, when they here peruse, as it is hoped they may, and meditate, as they ought, upon the solemn denunciation of these very amusements, by saints and doctors of the church of God? Good and faithful parents will read these pages with the deepest interest, and endeavor, at the same time, to impress the truths which they contain upon the minds of those entrusted to their care. Misguided men, blinded by the spirit of avarice, and who erect dancing halls in order that they may make a profitable traffic in the vices and follies of others, will not, of course, like this book; they will probably declaim against it as putting their craft in danger. Would that another Hulot amongst us had written a tract to serve as an antidote to counteract the baneful influences of liquor shops, as effectually as our author's labors tend to counteract those at work for the ruin of chastity in youth. Persons in the habit of spending Saturday nights in the dance house, or in the shops just mentioned, fall into grievous sins, and soon become hardened in guilt, and deaf alike to the voices of conscience and admonition. Parents, remiss in the duties of vigilance and correction discover, too often when it is rather late, the terrible results, in their offspring, of bad company, and the indulgence of inordinate passion.

When the virtues of obedience, reverence, and purity are lost, revolts against parental authority inevitably follow; for, without these, order and happiness cannot exist in the family, or in any condition of human life.

St. Alphonsus, in his "Rule of Life for the Father of a Family," directs, that "parents should forbid their children to go to dances."

The "Mission Book," recently published in New York, by the pious and exemplary Redemptorist Fathers, whose experience is most extensive and thorough among all classes of the faithful, and which Archbishop Hughes, in his approval of it, states, "has received the commendation of many distinguished prelates in Europe," uses this emphatic language: "Dances, balls, and plays are dangerous and ruinous for a young woman. In the voluptuous dance innocence dies, and on the way home it will be buried. The first step on the dancing floor is, for the greatest part, the first step towards seduction."

Servant maids, carried away by a passion for the excitements of parties and dancing, have been known to spend the earnings of a whole year in preparations for a single ball.

The writer knew a case of horrid cruelty, resulting in the death, by starvation of a parent, which was caused, or could have been prevented, were it not for this same passion. During the late famine in Ireland, a widow mother applied to her only daughter, at New York, for relief. The unnatural daughter, refusing to respond to the call of her poor mother, went on, as usual, spending all her wages at balls.

Volumes would be required to record the opposition to dances manifested by the most venerable and revered authorities. Benedict XIV. affirms, "On account of the manner in which it is now carried on, dancing is scarcely to be permitted, since, for the most part, it is the occasion of sin." "In general practice, every dance among persons of different sexes is to be prevented as much as possible; for, as they are now usually conducted, they are, for the most part, very dangerous. Hence parish priests and confessors should, to the utmost of their ability, avert their subjects and penitents from them. Thus commonly teach the doctors of our time, and the directors of souls." — *Gury's Moral Theology.*

Bishop Lefevre, the zealous and learned bishop of Detroit, in his Pastoral, *(Oct.,* 1850,) addresses thus the clergy and laity, in relation to an abuse prevailing in his, as well as in several other cities, where excursions, etc., are availed of to raise money for good and charitable objects:

"To our age is reserved the honor of adding to the dictionary of our language the word 'charity ball,' and of teaching that what dishonors God, blasphemes our religion, and places a stumbling block to a multitude of souls, who find in it both spiritual and temporal ruin, can be right, and even praiseworthy, on account of that relief which it may afford to the poor, etc.; in other words, that the end justifies the means, however criminal they may be in themselves, or in the circumstances attending them. You are well persuaded, and we loudly proclaim it, that you must give alms according to the precepts of our Lord; but remember well that this God, infinitely wise, cannot be indifferent to the manner in which you acquit yourself of this work of charity, in order that it may answer to His design, and be meritorious to you.

"For in order that any work whatever may be truly good, it does not suffice that it should be good under a certain relation, or in some of the circumstances attending it, but it must be good in every relation—in its object, which should be proportioned to the act; in its end and in its circumstances, which should all be in harmony with the act itself; in fine, in its intention, which should be nothing else than the goodness of the act. If one of these conditions be wanting, it not only ceases to be good, but it becomes vicious and detestable in the eyes of God—becomes a sin.

"After this, can we imagine that God will receive as righteous and meritorious an act of so-called charity, through this instrumentality of balls and dances, with all the dangerous and criminal circumstances that, especially in our days, accompany them? Is not this to overturn all the rules of Christian morality, and to insult God by pretending to perform an action agreeable to Him while we make use of the means which He has Himself forbidden; which the church, ever guided by the Holy Spirit, condemns; and of which even men of the world avow the fatal consequences from their own experience, and which pagans, despite the laxity of their morals, have marked with infamy?

There are no devices which the advocates of dances can contrive, sufficient to conceal the perils attending them, in our times, when the majority of young persons who frequent them are devoid of religion and morals. In Europe, as well as here, zealous pastors endeavor, with anxious assiduity, to withdraw Catholic youth from the dangerous vortex of these excitements. In the learned work of the Rev. A. Gillois, entitled *Theology for the Use of the Faithful or "Hist*orical, Dogmatical, Moral, Liturgical, and Canonical Explanations of the Catechism," several chapters are devoted to an exposition of the character of the various forms of the modern dance, and of the pernicious effects of these amusements.

This author classes the dance among the ordinary causes of impurity, and quotes some ordinances which even the civil authorities were forced to enact, in certain places in France, against nocturnal assemblies. The dance called there the galop schottischc was prohibited, and a fine imposed upon the musician, or the owner of the house in which such dance was held.

"There are dances," writes A. Gillois, "which should be absolutely forbidden, and in which one cannot take a part, not even for a single occasion, without incurring the guilt of mortal sin; such are the *waltz, the polka,* and the *schottische.*

. . . These dances are in their own nature bad, because the positions taken are improper; these should be forever banished from decent society, and it is difficult to understand how any female could submit to them, without abandoning the modesty which belongs to her sex. It may happen, too, in other dances, that the dress, gestures, and discourse may tend and strongly excite to voluptuousness; and from that moment they become an immediate occasion of sin, and consequently must be avoided. In public dances, such as, among the lowest classes of society, are held in liquor shops and saloons, or those of more respectable rank, termed dress and masquerade balls, and to which all who pay are admitted, there is a license so fearful allowed, that all persons unwilling to abandon them are to be regarded as unworthy of absolution."

"In balls and dances, the seven gifts of the Holy Ghost are effaced and lost. The first, which is the gift of *wisdom,* detaches us from the world, and gives us a taste of and love for the things of God; but the ordinary effect of the dance is to attach one to the world, and inspire a taste for its vanities and false maxims. The second, which is the gift of *understanding,* enables us to know and be impressed with the truths of religion; but the ordinary effect of the dance, by the bad affections which it awakens, is to lose sight of the truths of the religion which condemns and reproves these very same affections. The third, which is *counsel,* is the gift by which we know and choose what contributes most to the glory of God and our own salvation; but the common effect of dances is to make worldlings, at least, indifferent about God's glory, and neglect the care of their souls. The fourth, which is the gift of *fortitude,* enables us to surmount the obstacles of our sanctification; but the ordinary effect of the dance is, to weaken those who frequent it, so that they hardly think of God, and their love for him becoming cold, they cannot bear the least trial, and the slightest shock suffices to shipwreck them. The fifth, which is *knowledge,* is the gift by which we are enabled to see the way we should follow, and the dangers we should avoid, in order to arrive at salvation; but the ordinary effect of dances, by the excitements connected with them, and the giddiness which they cause, is to blind those who frequent them until they fall headlong into the snares of the devil. The sixth is the gift of *piety,* by which we embrace with pleasure whatever belongs to the service of God; but the ordinary effect of dances is, to make one fall, first into tepidity, and soon after into a neglect of the most essential duties of a Christian life. What taste, for instance, can a dancer have for prayer, frequent communion, decoration of altars, etc.? The seventh, the *fear of the Lord,* penetrates us with a profound respect and reverence for God, and makes us fear, above all things, to displease Him; but the ordinary effect of dances is to banish from the minds of those who frequent them every thought of God, and fear of His judgments, so that in a short time they are ashamed of nothing; therefore dances and balls efface, in worldlings, the graces of the Holy Ghost, and rob them of His sevenfold gifts."

This citation from the learned work of Gillois, approved as it is by high and eminent authorities, may serve to support the views of the author of this little treatise, which is now, for the first time, presented to the English reader, and in our country, in which, perhaps, after France, there is no other where its perusal is more needed. The translation was prepared hastily, by a talented young ecclesiastical student, previous to his setting out for Europe to complete his theological course.

Parents, especially in our cities, should not omit to place it in the hands of youth; they may read it too, themselves, with profit.

1

GENERAL CONSIDERATIONS ON DANCING. ITS OBJECT AND EFFECTS

Dances are assemblies of persons of different sex, principally young men and women, who move in measured pace, according to rule, to the sound of musical instruments, for the sake of procuring and imparting pleasure. Dances trace their origin from the rites of paganism, of which they formed the principal attraction. Men and women, heated by wine and lust, spent their time in revelry and in singing hymns in honor of Bacchus. The Egyptians made them an inducement to the worship of their god Apis. The Hebrews, who imitated the Egyptians around the golden calf, commenced that festival by a banquet, and prolonged it by licentious dances. At first, men danced to songs in the public places; afterwards they used flutes and other musical instruments. From the public places these amusements became fashionable in theatres, and thence found their way to the palaces of princes and nobles. Certain dances sometimes take place in cities, in the decorated and brilliantly-illuminated saloons of the rich. Here only people of fashion appear; young persons, in very elegant and often in very indecent attire, are commonly conducted to these dances by parents or friends.

Other dances take place on Sundays and festivals, in grog shops and in the dark haunts of infamy, the retreats of young libertines. These commonly commence in the day, and continue till late at night. Young females go there, and return only with their partners in the dance. During all this time the parents pursue their daily occupations, or remain indolent at home, and sleep tranquilly, without troubling themselves about the dangers to which the virtue of their imprudent daughters is exposed in these perilous assemblies. But in whatever place, whether in grog shop or in the gorgeous saloon, these profane amusements are held, the Holy Fathers have always regarded them as the work of the devil, who has made all pomp and vanity in order to ruin souls. Considering dancing as a mere exercise, we shall find it undoubtedly more ridiculous than dangerous. What, in fact, can be more laughable than to see dancers advance, fall back, bend the body, jerk it up again, and whirl around like birds struck on the head? If music had not lent the charm of its harmony to cover the folly and absurdity of dancing with an appearance of sense and propriety, and if people could only see the movements of dancers performed in silence, they could not help exclaiming with the greatest Roman orator, Cicero, that, *He who dances must be drunk or mad—* "*Nemo fere saltat sobrius nisi insanus.*"

What can be more repugnant to the taste of people of sense, than the motions, the gestures, and the jumps made in the dance? Louis Vivez, preceptor of Charles V., says, that some Spaniards, who visited France, were so frightened at seeing women dance, that they ran away, *believing them laboring under some extraordinary madness.* If the exercise which dancing affords were the sole object of those who frequent the ballroom and the dance house, if it offered them only the innocent pleasure which men can procure in the absence of women, and women in the absence of men, it would not exist long; to abolish it, it would suffice to make it the object of our ridicule, and compel young men and young women to dance separately, without seeing or speaking to each other. There are many who would never go to the dance house, if they did not expect to accompany thither, or did not hope to find there, the object of their passion. But we must not examine the mere external form of dancing; we must consider its aim and consequences. We see, then, that it comprises an infinite number of dangers, which are natural to it, which we cannot separate from it, without abolishing the whole form. It is almost always the rock on which innocence is wrecked; it is the *tomb* of shame, the theatre of all worldly passions, and the triumph of them all. We can easily see that it is a collection of all that is most dangerous to our salvation, and an assemblage of all temptations; that everything in it is injurious or poisonous: company, objects, conversations, occasions, the music,—all concur to seduce the mind and heart, and to stifle in them every sentiment of piety.

Why do people go to dances? Always to amuse themselves, to take part in the common pleasure, and contribute to it, and very frequently to expose themselves willfully to dangers, and to give freedom to passions which they have difficulty in taming even in solitude. *Who are the persons who go to such places?* They are partly *women,* who, adding the attraction of a fine dress to personal charms, do all in their power to make themselves agreeable and pleasing to men; they are partly *men,* who try to show these women that they are pleased with them and love them; young women, who devote their whole attention to ornamenting themselves with every thing most dangerous and seductive in nature and art, who use all the artifice possible in order to appear very attractive at these diversions, to excite more easily the attentions of young men, and to inflame in their hearts the fire of criminal passion; young men, who go there only to lay snares for the chastity of young women; who, the more easily to succeed in their wicked designs, whisper in their ears a thousand absurdities, a thousand extravagances and obscenities; who exaggerate their beauty and wit, flatter their self-love by giving them credit for qualities which they do not possess; young men, who disguise from these women their defects, or make them think they are models of perfection; who embrace them in order to excite their passions, or make them feel their ardent and impure love: such are the young men and women who frequent balls and dances, in order to make a reciprocal commerce in impurity, by indecent gestures, by impassioned embraces, lascivious looks, and immodest words. The ballroom is the rallying point of all that is most vicious, most immodest, most corrupt in all classes of society; the dance is the ordinary *rendezvous* of the vilest slaves of the most shameful passions, who communicate to each other the mortal poison with which their infected heart overflows; it is a fiery furnace, where everything burns with an impure flame, where all is a snare for chastity—that most valuable gem of all the virtues—that virtue which must be continually guarded in order to avoid its being entrapped. *Dancing* say the Holy Fathers, *is the work of the devil, and the theatre of hell.*

It cannot be questioned, says Madame Leprince de Beaumont, but that of all the desires that rule the heart of women, that of pleasing is the most violent; it is this desire which produces in them love of dress, jealousy, and vanity. But at balls this desire acquires new strength. It leads them to envy the lot of persons of their own sex, whom they see better dressed, or better dancers, than themselves; it makes them hate those whose society is more courted or sought after; in a word, this desire makes them sow discord among men, who often, in order to satisfy the vanity of a contemptible woman, quarrel and fight among themselves, and kill each other in duels.

If women were sincere, they would agree that the desire of pleasing and being preferred to others, rather than anything else, brings them to the ballroom. But among the great number of men whom they try to attract, there are always some who attract them in turn, and please them too much. As these women badly conceal the impression made on them by young men, the latter profit by it, by holding tender and impassioned discourses with them, the poison of which they swallow with a relish that they cannot always hide. If the effects of this passion are not seen immediately, they are not the less real or the less frightful.

As young persons of different sex are at all times and in all places occasions of sin to each other, it is especially at the dance that the occasion is most dangerous, the peril most imminent, and most difficult to be shunned. In the perilous occasions with which the world is filled, people are not always incited to sin by all their senses at once. If their mind is troubled by thoughts contrary to chastity, the heart does not feel at the same instant the fatal impressions. If their ears are sometimes flattered by tender discourses or immodest songs, their eyes are not always struck at the same time by the presence of seductive objects, so that if they are urged on to sin by one sense, the others can at least hinder them from yielding to the temptation; but in the dance young people are incited to sin by all their senses together. The senses are so many channels which the devil uses to pour, all at once, into their souls the poison which lust begets. Whilst their eyes are dazzled by the splendor and pomp displayed by the vanity of those composing these worldly assemblies, perfumes and odoriferous essences please the smell; their heart is a prey to the charms of all those seductive objects placed before them; their ears are pleased by the poisoned sweetness of licentious conversations that are being held, and by the harmony of voluptuous music, which seems to communicate to the objects assembled a new life and new attractions, in order to seduce them more easily, and entirely enslave their already softened and enervated hearts. As, while celebrating in the sanctuary the benefits of the Creator, music inflames the coldest heart with the fire of divine love,—as on the field of battle it communicates to the most timid an indomitable courage,— so also in the dance, by inflaming the heart with impure love, it fills it with lust, and strengthens this lust after it has been allowed to enter. If to all these dangers which beset young people in these pernicious assemblies, we add those which the tumult and agitation that reign in them, and the immodesty which everyone tries to show in his looks and by his deportment, naturally produce, we shall be forced to confess that it is almost impossible for young persons to resist long the attractions to lust, in a place where all inspires it; we must say that these diversions cause the love of the world and of creatures to enter sweetly and agreeably into the hearts of the dancers, and banish the love of God and of religious duties. Horrible corruption ensues, whose vapor clouds their minds, extinguishes the light of faith, and gives rise to irreligion and atheism; for *from impurity to impiety there is but one step!* When once you have fallen into this infamous passion, you have a thousand difficulties to surmount in your way back to virtue. If the acute remorse of a disturbed conscience may force you to shun crime for a moment, habit, which always rules, and the pleasures that you imagine are to be found in it, soon lead you back to your old course of life, and prevent repentance, without which there is no possibility of gaining salvation. When man has reached this degree of corruption, he cannot bear the thought of a just God, into whose hands he must fall after death; he wishes to smother those importunate qualms of conscience which trouble and imbitter the pleasures which he loves, and which he is unwilling to sacrifice. He endeavors to persuade himself there is no God, and consequently no hell; he sleeps in this foolish security, and is awaked only by the *heat of eternal flames.*

I ask, now, if we have not good reasons to say with the holy doctors and most famed theologians, that dancing is an infectious *sink of jealousy, rivalry, buffoonery, raillery, quarrels, obscenity,* and *impiety,* a *school* of *vice,* where one learns the art of *corrupting himself and of corrupting others?* What virtue is so strong as to be able to appear in the dance without running the risk of fading in the pestilential air exhaled from it?

If a religious woman should forget herself so far as to appear at a ball, would not such levity and imprudence give rise to the most malignant reflections? "If this person," most men would say, "does not conceal a corrupt heart disposed to deliver itself up to the most shameful disorder under affected modesty, she will soon find that it is impossible to throw herself into the bosom of corruption, and the most seductive temptations, without being infected; she may have been a chaste dove, she will soon have all the malice of the impure serpent." Would you not blame a woman who, having communicated in the morning, would go in the evening to a dancing party? Could you hesitate to say that she had gone to receive her Creator in the sanctuary only to be able to despise him, trample him under her feet, and sacrifice him to the devil? Can expressions strong enough be found to express the indignation we feel at the indignity offered to God? If it is acknowledged by everyone that balls are dangerous and criminal for a religious person, or for one who has received the bread of life, can they be innocent and without danger for one who loves them passionately, who frequents them with all the vain show of worldly pomp, with that air of levity which characterizes the professional dancer, who has little or no love of God, little fear of offending him, little anxiety for her salvation? Is it not evident that a giddy, careless young woman runs more danger in such places than a holy soul, opposed to vanity and worldly follies, and deeply endowed with the love of God? Will not the blow which wounds the one undoubtedly kill the other?

Whoever knows the true value and delicacy of chastity, that a too lascivious look, a simple desire, can destroy it, and is aware of the violence of the passions that conspire against it, will agree that it is not possible to go to dances and balls without exposing this virtue to the greatest dangers; that people never leave them without having either lost it or weakened it considerably. But if dancing is dangerous for everyone, it is especially so for young people, whose passions are most unruly and most destructive, as they take very little pains to restrain them.

For what should one do in order to restrain his passions? He should avoid the occasions which make them spring up, and refuse them the fuel which keeps them burning; but these are means which young persons do not wish to use. They know that nothing is more suitable for strengthening their passions than the frequenting of these worldly assemblies, where all glitters, where all seduces; this consideration does not prevent them from frequenting them whenever an occasion is offered; and, far from seeking to shun the seduction which they encounter there, they find no greater pleasure than when they deliver themselves up to it without reserve. Going forth from these haunts of lewdness, says St. Anthony, a thousand bad thoughts follow them step by step; they feel that their imagination steals from them in order to return to the scenes of their immodest pleasures. The objects which they have seen, the conversations they have heard, the embraces that they have received and returned, come into their head, seduce their heart, and fill them with the desire of returning; and, *in fact,* they return as often as possible. The excessive passion that they conceive for these foolish joys strips them even of a thought of avoiding them, makes them forget their most important duties, inspires them with disgust for the practice of piety, with a sacrilegious contempt for religion and its holy truths, a monstrous indifference for their salvation; it hardens their heart, and leads them to despair. Such are the sad fruits of dancing, and of the sins which it occasions. Ought we any longer to be astonished at the terrible maledictions launched forth against the daughters of sin and the vanity of their dress? They, as well as those who imitate them in this practice, invented by the devil, are threatened with becoming the prey and laughingstock of the conqueror, and with all the horrors which war and captivity bring with them. (Isaiah iii.)

What should we do to restrain our passions? We should employ watching, prayer, mortification, and penance; but young people regard these virtues as strangers to their age. Watching requires us to avoid sin and its occasions. Young people ought, therefore, to avoid the dance, which is always an occasion of sin to them, and which exposes them to many dangers, a single one of which would suffice to destroy their virtue. Dina, daughter of Jacob and Lia, impelled by an indiscreet curiosity, wished to go, on festival day, to the town of Sichem, to see the customs of the women of the country, and how they appeared in public. God, to punish her curiosity, and to give a warning to posterity, that young women could not avoid with too much caution all occasions of sin, permits the son of Hemor, king of that country, to see, and conceive for her a violent passion, of which she became the unfortunate victim. He had protected Sarah and Rebecca, ancestors of Dina, because they had not been curious about these things; but he did not protect Dina, because she had exposed herself to a danger that she ought to have shunned. It is thus that God abandons young persons who go to balls with intentions far worse than this young Israelite had. If he strengthens them against temptations which they try to avoid, but which, nevertheless, they experience, he withdraws his support from them when they seek to fall into temptation by choice. "*He that loveth danger,*" says our Savior, "*shall perish in it;*" we love it when we do not shun it; we love it far more when we seek it. All is danger in the dance: is it not to wish your own ruin to go to it? If chastity cannot be preserved without God's grace, if God gives his grace only to those who pray for it sincerely, can we be supposed to ask for it sincerely, or can we hope to obtain it, when we are disposed to go to the ball? When we ask his grace, what attention could he be supposed to pay to our request? What grace could that young woman expect who loves the pomps of Satan which she has solemnly renounced in baptism, who wishes to follow those customs of a perverse world which he has a thousand times cursed? If God would grant her any favor in such a case, would it not be that of avoiding dangerous amusements? Therefore, when she is disposed to frequent the dance, she takes care not to ask such grace from God, for she would be very sorry to obtain it. Can we be astonished, then, to see, reigning in towns and places where this abuse has taken root, a crowd of disorders unknown elsewhere?

The only precaution that we can take in order to avoid the snares of the impure spirit, is to keep away from balls and dances; for if St. Jerome, St. Arsene, St. Benedict, St. Francis, and so many other holy hermits, in their deserts, removed from every occasion of sin, were obliged to mortify themselves, by painful works and continual fasting, to throw themselves among briers and thorns, to plunge themselves into the snow and into frozen ponds, lying there entire nights in order to resist their rebellious flesh, worn out by perpetual mortification, how shall it be possible for young people, without strength and without experience, to resist the demon of impurity in assemblies where all is capable of inflaming the most icy hearts, of exciting the most shameful passions of a corrupt body, and of adding fuel to the devouring flame in young minds so easily mastered by their rising passions? How can people walk amid the flames of such a fire without being burned? With this general consideration on dances, which alone should suffice to make them be banished and despised in all places where Christianity is professed, let us pass to the proofs which support our arguments. I extract these proofs from the Holy Scriptures, the Holy Fathers, Holy Councils, and from the theologians most renowned for their piety and learning.

We hope that these collected proofs will enlighten the mind and change the heart of those who have been the advocates of dancing, solely because they have never sufficiently considered the evils of which it is the cause and the occasion.

2

DANCING CONDEMNED BY THE HOLY SCRIPTURES

The Holy Scriptures forbid us to regard too attentively persons of a different sex, as well as to converse too familiarly or act with levity with them. Now, all this takes place at the dance, not as being incidental, but as being its very source and essence.

With regard to lascivious looks, the Holy Spirit says, "Look not upon a woman that hath a mind for many, lest thou fall into her snares; gaze not upon a maiden, lest her beauty be a stumbling-block to thee; turn away thy face from a woman dressed up, and gaze not about upon another's beauty, for many have perished by the beauty of a woman, and thereby lust is enkindled as a fire." (Eccles. ix. 3, 5, 8, 9.) "Whoever," says Jesus Christ, "shall look on a woman to lust after her hath already committed adultery with her in his heart." (Matt v. 28.) How many adulteries of this kind are there not committed in dances, where people go only to see and to be seen, and very often to impart to others and receive from them the most injurious impressions, through lascivious looks, indecent behavior, and brilliant dress, which hardly covers the body, or, covering it with diabolical artifice, is sometimes more seducing than downright nudity!

If the Holy Ghost forbids us to look on a woman dressed up and fickle in her desires, and commands us not to gaze upon a maiden, is it not evident that he more strictly forbids balls, where numbers of giddy women and fickle maidens are assembled, and who occupy themselves only in displaying their charms, in order to attract the attention of young men, and to inspire them with criminal passions?

The Holy Spirit explains himself on the subject of a female dancer thus. He regards her as a very dangerous person, and wishes her to be avoided. "Use not much the company of her that is a dancer, and hearken not to her, lest thou perish by the force of her charms; for the conversation of these women burns as fire." (Eccles. ix. 4.) What can the partisans of dancing answer to these oracles of the Holy Ghost? What can they do better, in hearing them, than to bow to them in silence, to be docile and attentive to them, and to condemn what they condemn?

If all Christians would wish to do like holy Job,—set a guard on their eyes, to prevent them from too attentively regarding a maiden, for fear that her beauty might be their ruin,—it would not be possible to observe this in dances, since they cannot frequent them without gazing at those with whom they dance; for this is the first lesson which the teachers of this dangerous amusement inculcate to their unfortunate pupils.

We see, after what has been said, that the Holy Ghost not only forbids us to be in the company of female dancers, and to look attentively at them, but he forbids us also to listen to them, to converse with them, for fear that we may perish by the power of their charms, and be consumed by the fire of their corrupt conversations. He adds, "Tarry not among women; for from garments cometh a moth, and from woman the iniquity of man," (Eccles. xlii. 12-14;) that is to say, as the moth which is engendered in the garments is not perceived till the evil is done, so also the spiritual evil, which springs from conversations too frequent and too familiar with those of different sex, is not perceived at first, because it is still concealed in the thoughts and desires; but it is not slow to manifest itself in actions. It is for this reason that he adds, that a man who injures you, and thereby gives you an occasion for exercising your patience and temper, is better than a woman who serves you, and who, by her engaging manners, inspiring you with love for her, and causing you to fall into sin, becomes your confusion and shame.

The Holy Ghost, speaking of a woman who understands better the art of seducing men who have the imprudence to stop in her presence, and whose company and conversation are consequently more dangerous, says that, "Her lips are like a honeycomb dropping, and her throat smoother than oil. But her end is bitter as wormwood, and sharp as a two-edged sword," which kills in one blow both soul and body; that, "Her feet go down into death, and her steps go in as far as hell; they walk not by the path of life; her steps are wandering and unaccountable. Now, therefore, my son, hear me, and depart not from the words of my mouth; remove thy way from her, and come not nigh the doors of her house." (Prov. v. 3, 4, 6-8.) How many young women does not one find in dances, who are not, it is true, prostitutes, like those of whom Solomon speaks, but who at least are very giddy, very fickle, and "whose lips are like the honeycomb," because they are agreeable and seducing in their effeminate discourses! To go and dance with them, is it not to walk in the same road with them? Is it not to participate in their iniquity? Is it not to expose yourself to the danger of conceiving a passion for them, and sinking with them into hell?

If, as the Holy Ghost orders, one should not let himself be seduced by the artifices of a giddy, wicked woman, he should not go to dances where he meets numbers of them. In fine, the Holy Spirit forbids too free manners with persons of different sex, and says that it is not more possible to escape without defilement than to conceal fire in your bosom, or tread barefooted on burning coals, and not be burned. "Do not strive, do not drink, do not dispute with a woman," he says, "lest thy heart decline towards her, and by thy blood thou fall into destruction." (Eccles. ix. 12, 13.) Can anyone dance, and particularly *waltz,* with those of the opposite sex, without taking on them liberties infinitely more culpable than those the Holy Ghost here forbids? Is it not to free impurity from the shame which concealed it, to manifest it before the eyes of a crowd of spectators, who are so much infected with it themselves as to applaud its ravages? Can we not say, that the *waltz,* which, in the opinion of even the most careless men, can destroy the most rigid virtue, strengthens the corruption which it creates? That it is a violent poison, which kills on the spot the soul of young women and men, and sends them to the horrible flames of hell?

The dance not only is dangerous for our salvation, but it also makes it impossible for us to follow the advice that Jesus Christ and his apostles give us. Our Savior tells us to "watch and pray at all times, lest we fall into temptation." (Matt xxvi. 41; Luke xxi. 36.) The apostle St. Peter orders us "to be always on our guard against the devil, who goes about seeking to devour us." (1 Ep. v. 8.) But it is especially during the dance that the devil is most occupied in seeking to destroy souls, for then it is easiest for them to fall into sin. It is then also when prayer and watching are most necessary; but all we see there, all we hear and feel, takes away even a thought of these things. The soul is so debased that it is no longer itself, and finding itself in the midst of perils, it invites, as it were, the devil to come and take possession of it as his lawful property. St. Paul commands us "not to deliver our members to sin," (Rom. vi. 13;) but do we not act contrary to his command when we employ the feet in dancing, which God has given us to walk decently, and to go only where duty and necessity call us? Is it not almost to tread the gospel under foot, to violate the law of God, and give others an occasion for violating it? The same apostle exhorts us "to close our senses against the devil." (Eph. iv. 27.) And in the dance do we not open to him all the gates of our sense, and in particular our eyes and ears, as if to invite him to enter the soul without the least opposition? St. Paul further exhorts Christians to "mortify, therefore, their members, which are upon the earth; the fornication, uncleanliness, lust, evil concupiscence, and covetousness, which are in them," since "it is these passions which make the wrath of God fall on rebellious mortals." (Col. iii. 5, 6.) The dance, far from mortifying the members of the body, which are passions and vices, contributes, on the contrary, to give them more power and activity. Let any one examine himself after coming from the dance, and he will find that his passions are stronger, temptations more frequent, and that he has less strength to resist them. I appeal to those who have formerly loved this pernicious amusement, but whom grace has touched; they confess, weeping, that they have committed and seen committed by others, in the dance, innumerable sins.

"Love not the world," says St. John, "nor the things of the world. If any man love the world, the charity of the Father is not in him. For all that is in the world is the concupiscence of the flesh, and the concupiscence of the eyes, and the pride of life, which is not of the Father, but of the world." (I Ep. ii. 16.) If concupiscence is not of God, then all that strengthens it is not of God, but of the world. Now, nothing is more fit for creating and strengthening concupiscence than lascivious dances, which are so much frequented at the present day. Dances are, therefore, not of God, but of the world, which could not invent a more dangerous diversion, nor one more fit for seducing and destroying souls. Those who love these diversions passionately belong not to Jesus Christ, whose maxims are contrary to those of the world, and whose whole life was a manifest condemnation of such amusements as the dance.

Avoid it, then, as the rock on which your chastity will be wrecked. God has permitted many strong in virtue to be destroyed there before you, in order to teach the weak that the surest way to avoid the evil is to shun its occasions. We are not more holy than David, wiser than Solomon, or stronger than Samson; we know how great a number has been destroyed by frequenting the dance house or ballroom, and their occasions. The sight of Bethsabee made David commit adultery; Samson's love for Dalila caused him to lose his strength, and put him in the power of his enemies; the strange women whom Solomon loved corrupted his heart, and led him into idolatry. Who cannot tremble at the thought of these frightful examples? "If your right eye and your right hand scandalize you," says Jesus Christ, "pull out that eye, cut off that hand, and cast them far from you." (Mark ix.) It is evident that our Savior, in saying the right hand and the right eye, wished us to understand that we should sacrifice our dearest and most precious possessions or loves in order to avoid sin. In adding, that we should throw away this eye or this hand far from us, he means that we cannot avoid too much that which leads us into sin, which is the only earthly evil. As reserve in conversation, in looks, and in manners, is the only protection of chastity, a Christian, who wishes to preserve his virtue, must banish forever the thought of going to balls or dances, where it is impossible to have this reserve.

I demand, now, with St. Ephrem, of the most zealous partisans of dancing, how they will prove "that it is allowed to dance." What single one of the prophets has said so? What Gospel authorizes it? In what Epistle of the apostles is there a single word in its favor? To permit such a diversion to Christians, we must brand the law, the prophets, the writings of the apostles and evangelists, as full of errors; but if all the words of these holy books are true and inspired by God, as they really are, it is incontestable that Christians are prohibited from frequenting or enjoying the amusements of which we speak. "Yes, there is no safety for modesty," says St. Ambrose, "where this precious virtue has everything to fear from the attractions of pleasure." If Cicero, and the greatest lights of human wisdom, have said that drunkenness or folly is the foundation of the dance, the Holy Scriptures, where we read that St. John was put to death by the request of a dancer, show us one of the fatal consequences which this pleasure carries with it.

I know that the advocates of dancing are accustomed to cite the example of David before the ark of the Lord. If they give the name of *dance* to the action of David in this circumstance, they must at least agree that it was not a *dance* like that which we attack in this little book. "This holy king did not dance through love of pleasure," says St. Ambrose, "but through a spirit of religion; not to strengthen his passions, but to make his love for God more evident and public, and to publish his gratitude to him for his benefits, who was now crowning his wishes; not to make himself be admired by the spectators, but to humble and abase himself before God, in whose sight all are as nothing." Can we compare the dances of our times with that of David? Do people go to dances to humble themselves before the Lord, to give homage to his greatness and majesty, to manifest their gratitude to him for all his liberality? Do people sing holy songs, that elevate the soul, in our modern dance houses and ballrooms? On the contrary, do we not hear licentious airs and dissolute songs, which plunge the soul into the filth of sin, and inspire it with love for creatures? Are not men and women mixed up together in those hells? Are there not discourses and liberties permitted, the very mention of which make modesty blush? It is foolish, then, to pretend to authorize dancing, where there is not a thought of God permitted, by quoting the example of David, whose dance expressed the sentiments of the most lively gratitude and the most perfect piety towards his Creator.

3

DANCING CONDEMNED BY THE HOLY FATHERS AND DOCTORS OF THE CHURCH

The Holy Fathers who have been, each in his turn, the organs of the church, have spoken severely against dancing. "Young women who love the dance," says St. Basil, "lose the fear of God, and despise the flames of hell; far from pondering, in retirement, on that terrible day when the heavens will be opened, and when the sovereign Judge of the living and the dead will descend to render to everyone according to his works; far from endeavoring to purify their hearts from every bad thought, and effacing by their tears the sins they have committed, they shake off the yoke of the Lord, they trample under foot his holy law, they cast off the veil with which decency requires them to be covered; they expose themselves, without shame; to the eyes of men; they assume an impudent look, laugh immoderately, and act as becomes neither their age nor sex; they conduct themselves like those in transports of madness, and excite by their behavior the passions of young men." *(Hom. Inebriosos.)* Whether they act with the intention of exciting irregular passions, or do not, they are not the less culpable, for the evil is produced in either case. "It is by her dancing," exclaims St. John Chrysostom, "that the daughter of Herodias captivated the heart of Herod, who had the folly to promise, as a reward for it, to give her whatever she should ask; and she had the cruelty to demand from him the head of St. John the Baptist. It is the devil," he continues, "who made her dance so gracefully, and who made Herod fall into his snares; for he is always present where there is a dance; it is in such amusements that he is most pleased, and where he has the greatest ease in destroying souls. If dancing at the present day does not cause the death of St. John the Baptist, as that of the daughter of Herodias did, it causes a death far more sorrowful to the members of Jesus Christ. Those who dance now do not demand that the head of the holy precursor be brought to them in a dish, but they ask, for the devil, the souls of those present. If no daughter of Herodias appears in the dances of our times, the devil, in whose form, as it were, she danced then, is the spirit of them, and leads captive the souls of his dupes who frequent them." "This spirit of darkness," says St. Augustine, "takes, as the occasion may require, different forms to attack Christians. He had taken the form of a furious lion, when he incited infidel princes to murder them on scaffolds, burn them at the stake, and torture them on the rack; after the persecutions, he took the form of a serpent, which endeavors to seduce and deceive them." "As he cannot exercise his cruelty on their body, he destroys their souls by dances and lust; and the better to use his mortal poison, he conceals himself, and slips under the leaves of worldly pleasures," says the learned Gerson. "With what address does he not deceive you," says St. Ephraim, "and persuade you to do evil instead of good; to leave off dancing today in order to return to it tomorrow; to be today fervent Christians, tomorrow pagans, impious wretches, apostates, enemies of God! Do not deceive yourself; you cannot serve two masters at once; we cannot serve God and dance with the devil. Remember that the Savior has said, 'Woe to you who are in joy, for one day you will be in affliction and tears.'"

"Why do you try so much to procure pleasures? A slight cold may put an end to them; a single hour can separate you forever from those with whom you are accustomed to dance. In a single hour those feet which God has given you to walk modestly, and which you use so ill, may be immovable, stretched out stiff in death. Then all those who have been your companions in these diversions will abandon you. No one will be nearer to you now than the demons whom you have obeyed, and who await the consent of the Savior to carry your wretched soul into hell; for you cannot expect to rejoice with angels in heaven after having diverted yourself with demons on earth," says St. Peter Chrysologus.

"The devil," says Tertullian, "leads people no longer to the temples of idols, but to the ball, where one sees living statues, living idols, who try with all their charms to seduce the heart, and make it apostatize." If we find Christians in these profane assemblies, it is a mark that they are no longer true Christians; for can that which wounded the conscience of the primitive Christians be permitted to those of our days? Is not our holy religion as invariable in its morality as in its dogmas?

"The dance" says St. Charles, "is an ingenious invention for corrupting morals; it is the cause of bad thoughts, impure expressions, of adulteries, of the most shameful acts of impurity, of quarrels and murders; it turns away many persons from their religious duties, from prayer, holy reading, and makes them inattentive to the instructions of which they stand in extreme need. One cannot go there, continues this holy archbishop, "without frequently and grievously offending God. Can anyone desire his salvation, and expose himself to so many and so great evils, which are the unhappy fruits of dancing?" (*Actes des Conciles de Milan.*)

4

DANCES CONDEMNED BY THE HOLY COUNCILS

The council of Laodicea, held in the fourth century, permits a banquet to be given at a wedding, provided everything is conducted decently; it does not allow "that they act at it in a shameful and indecent manner, or *that they dance.*" (Concil. du Père Labbe, tom. i. can. 53.)

The third council of Toledo, in Spain, held A. D. 589, orders "that the irreligious custom, which the people have introduced, of employing their time in dancing and singing immodest songs on festival days, instead of assisting at the divine service, be entirely abolished; not only because they injure their own souls, but also because they disturb, by the noise made in them, the piety of more religious Christians." (Labbe, tom. v. can. 23.)

The council of Trulle (so called because it was held under the dome of the palace of the Emperor Justinian) declares "*that it condemns and abolishes the public dances* of women, as drawing after them many faults, and the loss of many souls." (Labbe, can. 62.)

The Roman council, held in 826, under Pope Eugene II., complains "that there are some persons who cause people to come on holydays, not to lawful and holy spectacles, as should be, *but to dance and sing immodest songs.* If those who act thus come to church with few sins, they depart with many." (Idem, can. 37.)

The Fathers of the council of Rouen, held in 1581, "condemn bad and indecent amusements, *dances,* as being full of folly; in a word, all that tends to impurity and the profanation of festival days." (Idem.) The council of Rheims, held in 1583, forbids expressly to profane holydays by *plays and dances.* (Idem.)

The councils of Tours and Aix, held the same year, forbid dances *under pain of anathema;* and they order clergymen to inform their bishops of those who will not obey this canon, in order that the bishop may pronounce the sentence of excommunication against the offender by name, (Idem;) "because," says the former, "it is against all reason and discipline for the faithful to allow themselves to be seduced, by the artifices and attractions of the devil, from attending to their duties and prayers on days that are intended for them to appease God's anger, and obtain pardon for their sins."

The council of Narbonne, held in the 17th century, forbids dancing, particularly on holydays, "for fear," says it, "that God may make the same complaint against us as he did formerly of the Jews, on account of the manner in which they celebrated their festival days, by declaring to them by the mouth of the prophet Isaiah, 'Your incense is an abomination in my sight; I cannot bear your Sabbaths and other festivals, where there is nought but iniquity and sin;' that is to say, I detest your festivals, although they come from myself; they serve no longer to honor me; but they are loved by you on account of the unworthy profanation you make of them, and the disorders to which you deliver yourselves on them." (Idem.)

If the councils which I have just cited insist on the abolishing of the dance, particularly on festivals and Sundays, it is because in former times they were only practiced on such days, as is now the case in country towns throughout Europe; but the reasons for which they condemn dances are not less for other days than for festivals, since at all times they are the source of an infinity of disorders, and always involve the same dangers.

5

DANCING CONDEMNED BY THE BISHOPS AND THEOLOGIANS OF THE CHURCH

At all times, the most renowned and zealous bishops have given pastoral instructions to the faithful, exhorting them to avoid dances. Vialart de Hersé, bishop of Chalons, no sooner was made head of his diocese, than he wrote a circular to all his curates, exhorting them to use every effort of their zeal, and all the resources of their ministry, in abolishing dancing. He commands them to refuse absolution to those for whom they are in the least an occasion of sin, unless they promise to stay away from them, and fulfill their promise; to reprimand them often in public, and in the pulpit, by representing to them vividly the fatal consequences of dancing, and commanding them to put a brazen wall between themselves and all such amusements.

The learned Gerson says, that all sins are in dancing, and that human weakness is so great, that the dances are the certain cause of a multitude of sins. (Tom. iii. p. 921.) The Catechism of the Council of Trent says, that bad books and bad songs are condemned no less than dances, as they equally lead to impurity. Vincent de Beauvais says, that people sin in the dance by all their members, and sacrifice them to immodesty; that the time of life is not a time for diversion, much less for such an immodest sport as the dance, but that our life is time for groaning and weeping; and that dances are a worship rendered to the devil, who is the inventor of them, and who excites us to frequent them.

St. Anthony, Archbishop of Florence, says, that those who deliver themselves up to this fatal diversion travel on the road to hell, and will arrive there unexpectedly at some future day, where the road ends. "We read in the Apocalypse," says this holy archbishop, "that, the angel having sounded the fifth trumpet, the depth of the abyss opened; there rose from the bottom a smoke like that of a furnace; there went forth from this smoke locusts, which spread themselves over the whole world, and which received the power of tormenting like the scorpions of the earth. These locusts were like unto horses prepared for the battle; and on their heads were, as it were, crowns like gold, and they had hair like the hair of women, and their teeth were as lions. These locusts are dancers; and the pit whence they come is the bottom of hell; for the love of dancing is inspired by the devil, whose residence is hell. The smoke of the furnace, out of which the locusts came, represents the spiritual vapors and the effects of impurity which have given birth to dances. The locusts, who had, as it were, crowns of gold and hair like women, and who were like horses prepared for fighting, signify that the devils make use of dancers of both sexes, who prepare themselves for the dance more than on any other occasion, in order to attack and seduce the servants of God."

"Those who deliver themselves to this pernicious amusement," says the same holy man, "by their act declare themselves enemies of Jesus Christ; for they act in opposition to the commandments and sacraments which he has instituted for the sanctification of sinners. First, they go against baptism, because they violate the solemn promises they made at it to renounce the devil, all his pomps and all his works. Can one dance without following Satan, who directs it, without being attached to his pomps, or without doing his works, which are sins? They act against confirmation, because, after having been marked by the seal of Jesus Christ, they dishonor him by indecent gestures and postures of the body in the dance, and show thereby that they glory in bearing the seal and character of the devil, from whom everything immodest comes. They sin against penance, because they put obstacles in the way of repentance and the sorrow which they should have for going to the dance house, or having been at the dance; they act contrary to the sacrament of the Eucharist, because, after having received Jesus Christ, they go to crucify him again in these worldly assemblies; they act against the sacrament of marriage, because the dance gives rise to thoughts and desires contrary to conjugal fidelity."

"O, if someone could open your eyes to see the immense number of demons mixed up with the dancers!" says Cardinal Bellarmine; "O, if someone could make you perceive with what zeal those demons attend on the men and women assembled at the dance, with what art they try to make passion for women spring up in the hearts of men, and for men in the hearts of women, the sparks, or rather the flames, of impure love, in order to make their hearts a furnace of concupiscence! O, if you could see how these malicious spirits rejoice at the sight of those whom they have led into sin, far from being so anxious to be present at balls and dances, you would shun them with horror."

"Avoid the society of those impure spirits who incessantly try to enkindle in the hearts of those around them the fire of lust. A young man cannot dance with a young woman without feeling the sparks of an impure flame. If adultery and fornication are sins, the dance must consequently be so, since it leads to them." (Bellarm. Sermon.)

"In fact, there is nothing in dances that does not exceed the bounds of modesty," says Petrarch; "they present a spectacle which cannot but displease chaste eyes; the action of the hands, the movements of the feet, the immodesty and impudence of the looks, show that there is some internal disorder in the soul; the least marks often show that there is something hidden in the heart. The motions of the body, the manner of being seated or reposing, the gestures, the laughs, the gait, the conversations, are so many signs by which we can tell what is passing in the soul. Those who have any love for modesty ought to allow nothing effeminate to appear in their manner, and ought not to love a diversion which leads, in the end, to impurity; for while dancing we think less about the present pleasure than what we expect to come: the freedom that one gives to his hands, to his eyes, to his tongue; the immodesty of the songs, the darkness, dispel the restraint which modesty inspires, and give loose rein to the passions. Take away impurity, and you will have destroyed dances. It is the levity of our mind that makes the body so light, and gives it the power of making the motions necessary for dancing; so that it is properly to the dance that the words of the Psalmist can be applied: *"In circuitu impii ambulant"*—the wicked walk in a circle. M. de Roquette, Bishop of Autun, wishing to give his people an instruction on dancing, consulted a man, who, by his character and condition, was far from condemning these diversions; I mean the Count of Bussy-Rabutin, so remarkable for his wit and disgraces. "I have always considered balls dangerous," says he; "it is not my reason alone that makes me condemn them, it is also my experience; and, although the testimony of the Fathers of the Church may be very strong, I hold that, on this point, that of a courtier ought to be of far greater weight. I know there are persons who run less danger in these places than others; nevertheless, the most passionless are excited in them. They are usually young people who compose these balls, who are almost unable to resist temptation in private; and how can they resist it where the most beautiful objects—torches, violins, and the agitation of the dance—would enkindle passions in anchorites? Old people, who would go to balls, would be ridiculed for doing so against their conscience, and young people, to whom propriety permits this, must not only act against conscience, but expose themselves to great dangers. Therefore I maintain, that no one calling himself Christian should go to the balls or dances of our age; and I believe that clergymen would do right to oblige parents and masters to keep their children and servants from balls and dances." It is not a priest who speaks here, but it is a man of the world, a courtier; his testimony has the more weight, since he is more interested to speak entirely different. It is only the force of truth which compels him to condemn so sternly the ball and dance.

St. Eloi, Bishop of Noyon, does not content himself with only condemning them; he employs the pain of excommunication against dancers, which is the greatest the church can make use of against those who obstinately persist in error, or irregularity of conduct. Preaching one day in a parish near Noyon, he strongly condemned dances, which were the cause of great disorders to the inhabitants. The latter, not being able to suffer themselves to be stripped of the amusements which their forefathers practiced, and which they held from time immemorial, disobeyed the bishop, and resolved to kill him if he spoke any more of them. Their threats did not intimidate the holy pastor, who burned with the desire of shedding his blood for his flock, and who longed for the glory of becoming a martyr. The following year, he preached, on the anniversary of the former day, on the same subject, with still more vehemence than before. His zeal was met with injuries and outrages; the people talked of massacring him; but the veneration of his sanctity was so great, that no one dared raise his hand to strike the holy man. St. Eloi, seeing that his exhortations did not produce the desired effects, "gave," through excommunication, the most obstinate and hardened "to the devil, to mortify their flesh, that their soul might be saved on the day of the Lord." These are the words of St. Paul, pronouncing excommunication against the incestuous Corinthian. There were more than fifty servants of Archambaud, mayor of the palace, who immediately found themselves in the power of the devil, and taught others by their example to fear the judgments of God, in those of his ministers. Their pains and humiliations lasted a whole year. The holy bishop cured them only on the following festival, after having received their submission and that of all the inhabitants. Terrible example, which shows how displeasing dances are to God, and how blind and guilty those are who frequent them contrary to their pastor's advice!

In fine, there is scarcely a book on piety, whose author does not condemn dances and balls, and exhort the faithful to avoid them.

ST. FRANCIS DE SALES IS NOT FAVORABLE TO DANCES

Those who defend dancing are accustomed to oppose to us the authority of St. Francis de Sales; but, even though it were true that this saint had said something favorable to dancing, we would, nevertheless, not be justified in thinking it lawful; for we must not prefer the opinicn of one doctor, who can be deceived, however holy and remarkable he may be, to the infallible authority of the Holy Scriptures, of the Holy Councils, and all the Holy Fathers. But it is clear that this holy bishop has decided nothing in this matter contrary to the spirit of the church and tradition. If he appears to grant some things, it is in order that we may be converted more easily, and our minds less offended. When he says that the dance is not bad in itself, he considers it in a light in which it could be harmless, and not as it actually is in practice; for he declares afterwards that it is so conducive to evil by its occasions, that the soul is exposed to great dangers in it; that the darkness and other dangerous accompaniments make it suitable for sin; that the lateness to which it is continued makes us lose a part of the following day, which we owe to the service of God; that it is extreme folly to make night day, or day night, and to neglect works of piety for the purpose of obtaining foolish pleasures; that vanity and envy are brought to it by trying to outvie others; and that this vanity is such a great inclination to dangerous and culpable loves that *amours* are its ordinary consequences.

"I say of balls," adds this holy bishop, "what doctors say of mushrooms—the best are not good; so also the best balls are by no means good. Mushrooms attract the infection and venom of serpents which approach them; so also these nocturnal assemblies are filled ordinarily with the vices of this life; and because their appearance, their tumult, and the license which reigns in them excite the imagination, disturb the senses, and open the heart to pleasure, if the serpent whispers a sensual word or some flattery in the ear, if you are surprised at the look of the basilisk, your hearts are entirely disposed to receive his poison. These ridiculous but dangerous diversions," he continues, "dispel the spirit of devotion, weaken the power of the will, freeze the love of God, and awake in the soul a thousand sorts of bad dispositions. For this reason one should never frequent them, even in necessity, without great precautions. People should never go to them, when it is possible to keep away, unless prudence and discretion require that through politeness for society they should be present." But it rarely happens that people are unable to refuse, unless they willingly give occasion to be so, by not taking the precaution to avoid the society that would ask them to frequent such places. If anyone goes to a ball, being capable of avoiding it, he formally breaks the command of the great bishop. If a person is absolutely unable to refuse to go to a ball or dance, he should take the following precautions, which he prescribes:—

If it is necessary to eat mushrooms, one ought, by his advice, to season them well, and eat few of them, otherwise many will be poisonous; so also, if one is compelled to go to a dance, he must stay but a short time at it, and it must be seasoned in all its forms by good intention, by modesty, dignity, and decency, and one should stay there as short a time as possible, for fear that the heart might be attainted.

"As after having eaten mushrooms," he continues, "one must drink sweet wine, in order to destroy their dangerous effects, so also, after having been present in these assemblies, recourse must be had to holy and lively considerations, to prevent the dangerous impressions that the vain pleasure would make on the heart." "You ought to consider," he says, "that while you are dancing, many burn in hell for sin committed at dances and on their account; that many pious persons are at the same hour singing the praises of God and prostrate before him, beholding his beauty; that their time has been far better employed than yours; that millions of persons have suffered from horrible diseases, and have died in violent agonies, and that one day or other you will groan as they, while others will dance as you do now; that while you dance, you displease our Savior, the Blessed Virgin, and the saints who are looking at you; that your lifetime is passing, death is approaching; lastly, you ought to consider that you are nearing the frightful boundary between time and eternity, heaven and hell."

"These are the considerations which I suggest to you; but God will cause others to rise up in your minds if you have his holy fear."

I demand now if it is showing one's self favorable to balls to say that the best are not good; that they are so conducive to sin that the soul is exposed to great dangers in them; that they attract the vices and sins of this life; that the jealousy, quarrels, foolish loves which they produce excite the senses and dispose the heart to receive the poison of passions. Is it eulogizing them to say that they dispel the spirit of piety, weaken the will, make our love for God grow cold, awake in the soul bad dispositions? That they are the cause of the damnation of many souls, and that they displease our Savior, the Blessed Virgin, the angels and saints?

According to this great saint, one should not go to dances in necessity, without great precautions; but does this necessity exist for the number of young women and men who run to them madly on every occasion, and pass part of the night at them? Do they take the precautions that St. Francis de Sales prescribes? To those who pretend that these diversions are very innocent, and that there is no need of taking any precautions,—to those who go to these places of pleasure to fill themselves with agreeable ideas, and not to be filled with thoughts proper for exciting themselves to sorrow,—I put the question. In fine, he who would go to balls with the sole intention of observing all the conditions that St. Francis de Sales exacts, would find so little pleasure in them that he would not be tempted to return thither a second time. It is to be believed that the lady whom the holy bishop permitted to go to the dance on condition of thinking on death while she remained at it never willingly or frequently made use of his permission. In fact, we must agree that if one went to balls only when St. Francis de Sales permits, and only on the conditions he lays down, he would not commit much sin at them. Balls would be then places of repentance and mortification, rather than places of pleasure. Then those giddy, passionate young people who go to them with evil intentions would soon disappear, no longer to frequent the ballroom and dance house. No longer finding food for maintaining the corruption of their hearts, they would seek elsewhere diversions more agreeable to their evil inclinations. It is clear that the retreat of these would abolish dancing, and no longer give occasion for condemning it for its pernicious effects on society in every country where it prevails.

7

SUPERIORS, WHO FORBID DANCES, SHOULD BE OBEYED

If, after the authority of the Holy Scriptures, Holy Fathers, rules of the councils, and decisions of the theologians, anyone still presumes to enjoy the wicked pleasure of dancing, he shows by his conduct that he respects very little what is most pious and remarkable in the church. We should obey all the directions of superiors which are lawful and tend to the glory of God and welfare of souls. The bishops, assembled in council, were the lawful superiors of the faithful; the judgments which they have expressed against dancing had no other end than to guard them from sin, and from whatever would hinder their salvation; therefore it is unlawful to resist their authority.

If all the doctors unanimously decided that a certain article of food was poison, would it not be rejected with horror? The principles by which the bishops decreed that dances are dangerous and fatal to souls, are far more certain than those of doctors.

Should more precautions be taken to preserve a body which one day we must lose, than to save a soul which is to exist forever? It is God himself who has revealed in the Holy

Scriptures, and by the constant tradition of the Holy Fathers, that dances effect the ruin of those who love them and are unwilling to renounce them; we should therefore shun and condemn them, in order to render homage to God's infallible truth, since he can neither deceive nor be deceived.

8

DANGERS OF PUBLIC DANCES

Public dances would not be permitted, were it not that some of those who compose them prevent many sins which otherwise would be invariably committed in them. But these persons are often so immodest, and sometimes so corrupt, that they pay no attention to the criminal liberties taken before their eyes; or, if they do pay the least attention to them, it is for no other purpose than to laugh at them and to applaud them. I agree that there are many balls where no one would dare to take these revolting liberties, which shock those of the slightest modesty; but others are taken in their stead, which, although trivial in appearance, are in fact wicked, very culpable, and reprehensible before the eyes of God.

Even if a young man takes some slight liberties, which are the foundation of mortal sin, nevertheless, he does not lose the esteem of those present, whose only object is being diverted, who are filled with the same sentiments as himself, and who, perhaps, are disposed to do like him. These persons, far from making a crime of this kind of familiarity, regard it, on the contrary, as very innocent politeness, and necessary to enliven society; they deem him amiable only in proportion as he distinguishes himself by his levity.

This want of modesty and delicacy opens the way to a multitude of external and internal disorders. His actions are representatives of his thoughts; he forms intrigues and dangerous connections, and bad habits are strengthened. Young women, by their giddy behavior, indelicate gestures, and immodest looks, create, in the hearts of those who behold them, the poison of crime, and lay snares for the imprudent young men who compose these dangerous assemblies. They assist the devil in doing evil, and leading souls away from Jesus Christ, which he has redeemed by the price of his blood.

But, you will say, balls in high society, which are frequented only by rich persons and those who are well educated, do not offer all these dangers; the surveillance that one has over the other banishes all kinds of disorder. But can this surveillance extend to the heart? Does it protect the soul from the poisoned arrows which the seductive objects assembled hurl at it? Does it render the heart insensible to the attractions of these girls and women, who display themselves in a gaudy dress to receive the homage and sacrilegious incense of adoring fools? Does this surveillance repress bad thoughts, and the consent given to them from the heart? Or does it prevent the mind from consenting in secret to the indulgence of the thoughts which the dance created?

If fear hinders a young man from manifesting his feelings, his soul is not the less free from bad desires, nor less seduced by the beauty of a young woman, as the heart of Holofernes was captivated by the beauty of Judith, and that of a Sichemite prince by the charms of Dina.

I say the same thing of the presence of parents; if it

hinders their children from extreme excesses, it is unable to prevent the too subtile poison of impurity from penetrating into their hearts by their eyes and ears, to repress thoughts and desires; desires of the flesh which escape the most clearsighted. What use is it to appear pure in the eyes of men, if one is not so in the eyes of *him who examines the heart and reins, and whose observation nothing can escape?*

When Jesus Christ, with the gospel in his hand, shall judge all men, will give rewards to those who followed him, and chastise those whose conduct has been opposed to his law, he will regard as guilty of *adultery,* and punish as such, *all those who have looked on a woman to lust after her.*

9

DANGERS OF PRIVATE DANCES.
CIRCUMSTANCES WHICH RENDER
THEM MOST CRIMINAL

The Bible, the Holy Fathers, and theologians make no difference between public and private dances; they teach unanimously that they are equally dangerous and illicit. Besides, private dances expose to the same dangers; they present the same occasions of sin; we can even say that the persons who compose these domestic assemblies, being freed from the reserve which they are obliged to observe in public assemblies, make their heart more open to destruction from dangerous objects. In a public assembly a young woman fears all eyes, because she knows that all present observe everything and pardon nothing; that a gesture, a glance, will be the object of severe criticism; but in these select assemblies she is not so reserved, because she fears opinions less. We cannot but agree that this species of liberty, unbridling her passions, and giving them supreme power, renders these far more dangerous for her than public dances.

If dances are criminal at all times, they are particularly so on Sundays and holydays; for God commands us not to work on these days, in order that we may have time to serve him. But how do licentious dances, which occupy a great part of the day, whose natural and inevitable effect is to excite the soul with violent passions, awaken in it the love of the world and destroy that of God, agree with the service of the Lord?

If a person were to make the house of God a den of debauchery, to drink and eat out of the sacred vessels, on the altar where the holy sacrifice is offered, who would not be horrorstricken at the sight of such a profanation? Are not Sundays and holydays consecrated to God as well as churches or altars, and vessels destined for the holy sacrifice? Why, then, are people less afraid to profane them by dances incompatible with the service of God? Would it not be better to work, sowing or ploughing, during these holydays, than to deliver one's self up to such criminal amusements?

It would be better to dig all day than to dance, says St. Augustine—*"Melius tota die foderent quam tota die saltarent."*

I know that some relaxations are necessary for people who have worked hard all week; but there must be a distinction made between dangerous amusements and those that are innocent: as nothing is innocent in the dance, as chastity runs nowhere more danger, it ought to be absolutely renounced. St. Paul permits us to enjoy ourselves, but in the Lord, in order that all men may see our modesty; but is it possible to dance without renouncing this virtue and trampling it under our feet?

If we were pious Christians, worthy of our name, we would be glad that the interruption of our ordinary labors gave us leisure to attend the holy mass devoutly, or to go to vespers, to say certain prayers, which we had not time to say the rest of the week; and then, if any more time remained, we would create some pleasant but innocent diversions. Can we not divert ourselves with wise and virtuous friends, who are sincerely attached to us? What is more pleasant for fathers and mothers than to find themselves surrounded by children who love them? What is more agreeable to a husband, who wishes to live chastely, than the presence of a wife who tries to please him? Let us imitate Jesus Christ, the Founder of our faith, who loves to receive our tears and mournings, but who is insulted by our immodest smiles; he does not desire that lips which have received his grace should be disturbed by a movement unworthy of a God-made man. Let us listen to God, who speaks to our hearts, and penetrates them with the fire which made David leap with joy in his prayers; from this joy spring up in the soul that exuberance of feeling which the consciousness of having done right creates, that sublime pleasure which the world does not understand, an unchangeable repose in the joy of a pure conscience, and sweet hope of possessing God; no music, no songs, no diversion, possess this great happiness.

But, it will be said, if young people are not allowed to dance, they may do worse: woe to those who do evil! A greater evil does not excuse a less; we cannot even approve of the smallest, since we are commanded to avoid all. Would it not be the height of folly to believe one's self authorized to commit a slight fault because a great one is forbidden, or to commit a great one because a small one is condemned? To think or act thus shows that your eyes are shut to the truth, and that you are determined to commit evil on every favorable occasion.

A second circumstance which renders dances more dangerous and criminal, is when they are held at night. Everyone knows that darkness, being an enemy of modesty, and a friend of crime, emboldens the most timid to execute the criminal projects which they have formed. How many persons permit and receive, under favor of the darkness, criminal liberties which they would not dare to countenance in daylight, through a remnant of modesty or fear of men! Nothing is more opposite to this rule of St. Paul than night dances: *"Walk soberly and modestly, as in the daylight."* (Rom. xiii. 13.)

A third circumstance which makes dances more culpable, is when they are attended by persons disguised; if the darkness of the night gives more boldness for committing wicked deeds, this boldness is naturally increased when we are confident of being unknown under a mask, or other disguise. But the most dangerous manner of being disguised is when the dress of a different sex is assumed. God forbade his people in the strongest terms to do so; this prohibition regards Christians as well as Jews, and is far more binding on us, who, living under the law of grace, are obliged to greater holiness. "A woman," says the Lord, "shall not assume the dress of a man, nor a man the dress of a woman; the one that does so is abominable in the sight of God." (Deut. xxii. 5.) In fact, how many sins does not this change of dress occasion! A woman, by changing her dress, strips herself of modesty and chastity, which are the ornaments of her sex; and a man, by assuming the dress of a woman, gives us reason to fear that he is effeminate and licentious, and feigns a change of nature which is abominable before God.

A fourth circumstance, rendering dances especially criminal, is when they are held on holydays, fasting days, and particularly during the holy season of Lent, which ought to be exclusively devoted to mortification, to weeping, and grief. It is for this reason that the church has denied us our usual food. All that is mournful or afflicting is joined to fasting now, as well as when sackcloth, ashes, and tears were its accompaniments among the Jews; and as it is an expression of the grief of the church, in the season when she lost her divine Spouse, conformably to these words of Jesus Christ, "The friends of the bridegroom do not mourn while the bridegroom is with them; the time will come when the bridegroom will be taken away, and then they will fast," (Matt. ix.,) we see that mourning and fasting ought to be characteristic of the days on which the church mourns the death and absence of her divine Spouse. She has always interdicted, and still interdicts, even innocent sports during this holy time, because they do not become the solemn mourning obligatory on all Christians. But by holding these dangerous amusements at all times, we withdraw from the authority of the church, which regards rebel Christians as heathens and publicans. To do this is in a manner to rejoice with Satan at the death of Jesus Christ.

10

CUSTOM CANNOT JUSTIFY DANCING

Since dancers can find no solid reasons for defending their favorite amusement, they support themselves by appealing to custom, which has established dances everywhere; they are pleased to think that the more dancing is extended and frequented, the less dangerous it becomes. "Woe-creating torrent of custom," exclaims St. Augustine, "where are all those who resist thee? Shall we then never see thee dried up? How long wilt thou sweep the unfortunate children of Adam into that deep, stormy sea, from which even those who hold to the wood of the Savior's cross have difficulty to save themselves? How many sins would be excusable, if custom were a lawful excuse! Blasphemy, theft, impurity, adultery, could not be crimes any longer, because there have always been many blasphemers, thieves, libertines, and adulterers. What would become of the law of God, if custom, which is often contrary to it, were the rule of conduct? Follow not the multitude in doing evil, says Jesus Christ; the many go by the broad road that leads to hell." "A bad custom," says Tertullian, "is established by ignorance and libertinism against truth and God, who is truth itself. For this reason, no space of time, no authority of men, no national privileges, have been able to render a custom legitimate which has not justice or truth as its foundation."

It was almost a universal custom among the Israelites to adore the golden calf of Jeroboam, king of Israel; but Tobias alone, of all the others, went to Jerusalem to adore the Lord in his temple. This custom, so opposed to the law of God, made then no impression on the mind or heart of the young Tobias. Why should custom sway us? Do we not owe to God the same fidelity as this holy man? Is it more lawful for us than for him to fall away from virtue, by following a custom which is contrary to God's law?

To enjoy dancing undisturbed, people use the authority of certain confessors, who allow it or oppose it very feebly; they prefer the authority of these to that of the Holy Fathers of the church, as if the former were more skilled in guiding souls. But does not our Savior warn us of false prophets? Does he not say that if "the blind lead the blind, both fall into the ditch"? Achab, king of Israel, was unwilling to listen to the only true prophet who had the courage to speak the truth; he preferred to listen to the false prophets who concealed it from him through complacency, and thus engaged him in an enterprise which cost him his life. Is not this the unfortunate disposition of many Christians, who, secretly enemies of truth, which combats their vices and errors, consult only those who may give a favorable response to their passions? Do they not deserve to be deceived, like Achab? "Because men have not received nor loved truth," says St. Paul, "God will send them a spirit of error, so that they will believe a lie, in order that all who have not believed truth, and who have consented to iniquity, may be condemned." (Thess. xi.) Whatever attempt we make to reconcile truth with our passions and interests, we may easily succeed in concealing it from us, but never in destroying it; and we will not escape having it for our judge.

11

DANCES FORBIDDEN AT NUPTIALS

The dance is forbidden in wedding festivities as well as on other occasions, for we should never expose ourselves or others to an occasion of sin. But is it not to be feared that young people, who are already excited by wanton songs which they have sung or have heard, by the licentious conversations which are held on the occasion of a marriage, by excess in drinking, which is of but too frequent occurrence at weddings, will allow themselves to be ruled by the pleasure they feel in the sight of each other, and by the familiarities mutually permitted? Is it not equally to be feared that the young men present may give the impure spirit an opportunity of insinuating himself into the souls of the young women, and mortally wounding their chastity? Nothing is more opposed to the sanctity of marriage than the dance. God has established this union not only to propagate the human species, but also to extinguish the fire of concupiscence, and to be a powerful preservative against its fatal effects. But does not sad experience prove that the dance serves only to render the fire of lust more lively, and consequently its effects more fatal? When young married persons have promised before God, and when he has blessed their union, religion does not hinder that there be a reunion of parents and friends, on the occasion of this holy ceremony, and that even some amusements be allowed, provided they be conducted modestly and soberly; but if, after such a holy action, they deliver themselves up to lascivious dances, they show by their conduct that they have no love of God, that it is banished from their heart, and they invite the devil to take possession of their souls.

For what purpose is dancing held at weddings? Is it to render them more magnificent? But nothing is more proper to embellish them than virtue. Is it to procure more pleasure? But there are no greater pleasures than those which leave no remorse. Is it to excite the passions? But marriage is established to calm them. Do you not see that the devil has introduced dances at nuptials only to create evil from good, and to embolden you to violate the law of God?

O you, who sully the sanctity of your marriage by criminal dances, fear lest God, aroused by your insult, may change into chastisement what he had granted you as a remedy! Fear lest your union, the commencement of which you celebrated with profane and criminal amusements, may be, by the just punishment of God, a source of miseries and grief. Jesus Christ was present at the marriage feast of Cana with his disciples; he will be present at yours, if you banish from them dances and other amusements which he condemns. He did not raise to life the daughter of Jairus till the musicians were driven out; he will not bless or sanctify your marriages until you banish from them those pleasures which inflame the passions, and voluptuous songs which excite them.

12

IT IS FORBIDDEN TO BE PRESENT AT DANCES

To be spectators at dances is forbidden, as well as to dance ourselves; for, to take pleasure in beholding others dance, is to give dancing our approbation. St. Paul declares that we must condemn the works of darkness, and take no part in them; for not only do the evil doers merit death, but also those who favor them. Besides, if one experiences pleasure in seeing others dance, he will not long refrain from dancing himself; if he has, up to this moment, a repugnance to doing so, he will easily be swayed by the examples of others to love this amusement, and participate in it, since it can be done with decency in the world's opinion. Lastly, we cannot be present at dances without witnessing many familiarities and criminal liberties permitted by those assembled. What more is necessary to produce in the soul bad thoughts and desires, which we cannot call unwilling, since we love what causes them?

If you find yourself in a society where all are decided on dancing, you must, if possible, withdraw quickly; if you have sinned in being present, do not add to your errors by participating in sinful actions, or favoring them by your presence.

You have sufficiently satisfied friendship by remaining with your friends only as much as your duties and salvation require; but friendship cannot force you to participate in the vices or faults of any one whomsoever: all that can be required lawfully of you, is, not to violate the promises you made in baptism.

13

DANCES ARE MORE DANGEROUS THAN THE SOCIETIES OF THE WORLD

If saints have not been so severe on worldly societies as on dances, it is because the latter were seen to possess far more dangers than the former.

We must nevertheless say that people run great dangers in worldly societies; that they frequently sin in them, when not present at them through religious motives, and even that there are some persons who, on account of their weakness, are obliged to keep away from them, because they give occasions of sin, while others, more strong in virtue, are not at all exposed. But as dances are, for the young, almost always an occasion of sin, they should never frequent them.

If in anything the good surpasses the evil, it may be admitted by cautioning about the evil; but when the evil surpasses the good, the thing must be rejected. It is on this principle that moralists forbid balls and dances, yet allow other assemblies. The dangers of other societies are not to be compared with those of dances. It is sometimes useful to be in society for business, for maintaining or establishing peace and union in families, but it is never necessary nor useful, but always dangerous, to be present at dances.

14

DELUSION OF THOSE WHO THINK THEY DO NOT SIN AT DANCES

Many persons pretend to have been at dances, and never to have experienced any of the bad effects attributed to dancing; but these persons do not watch sufficiently over their heart to perceive all the evil that works in it; they do not fear sin enough to be alarmed at what leads to it: provided that they avoid the external faults, always gross and revolting, they think they have escaped all the dangers of dancing. They regard the immodest thoughts and desires which spring up at dances only as light sins, to which the Lord pays no attention. Nevertheless, it is bad thoughts and desires, and internal consent which we give to them, that form, in reality, sin; for a wicked action, which we could not prevent, to which we did not willingly expose ourselves, and to which we did not consent, does not sully the soul which has had no part in it, and consequently is no sin; but bad thoughts and bad desires blacken the soul, kill it, and make it fit for eternal chastisements in hell. If a young woman looks on a young man *to lust after him,* she has already committed sin in her heart; if, according to the divine oracle, it is the same with respect to a young man looking at a woman, how many sins of thoughts and desires do the young persons of both sexes commit at dances, although they do not commit a single wicked action!

Nevertheless, I will suppose for a moment, what I have much difficulty to believe, that people never have suffered any spiritual damage from merely frequenting dances; supposing this, I say with St. John Chrysostom, "Is it not certainly a great loss and injury to your soul and salvation, to employ so ill a time of which all the moments are infinitely precious to you, and to make it a subject of scandal to others?" For when leaving these diversions, though even yourself have not been injured by them, are you not guilty of inspiring others, by your example, with a greater love for these dangerous pleasures? On this account all the disorders which spring up in regard to others, weaker than you, recoil on your head; for since, if no one would frequent dance houses, there would be no dances, it follows, that being a mere looker on is as bad as to participate in the amusement, because our presence makes dancing be kept up, and the spectators will go to hell, as well as those who sin by joining in the amusement. Therefore, even though you could dance without injuring your chastity, still you would deserve severe punishment, for having contributed to the ruin of others by your bad example. Certainly, however chaste you may be, you will be much more so by avoiding these dangerous pleasures. Let us not argue uselessly then, and let us not imagine vain excuses or defenses which have no weight before God. Our greatest defense is in avoiding this furnace of Babylon, and flying, like the chaste Joseph, this Egyptian seducer, when, to escape her wiles and hands, it becomes necessary to abandon all, even our clothes. By doing so we will procure true and solid pleasures by peace of conscience, which will no longer be troubled by remorse; we will spend in this world a pure and chaste life, and obtain in heaven life eternal by the grace and goodness of our Lord Jesus Christ.

15

PASTORS OUGHT TO OPPOSE DANCING

The pastor who has zeal for the glory of God and salvation of his neighbor, cannot behold without the keenest grief the frightful disorders which dances create, the outrage done to the Lord by them, and the multitude of souls they send to hell. He will not be content with solely condemning them; he will also employ all the authority which his character gives him, in order to destroy them, after the example of the saints who have preceded him in the pastoral career, and who were not afraid to expose themselves to raillery, to the censure and persecution of the world, when it became necessary to root out such a pernicious abuse. "I know," said St. John Chrysostom, "that by condemning dances, and wishing to abolish them, I will appear ridiculous to many, and that I will be accused of want of spirit and sense; nevertheless, I cannot keep silence, for all that. Perhaps that if all do not profit by what I believe myself obliged to say, at least some will be converted, and will prefer to be mocked at by us than to mock and laugh at us with a laugh worthy of eternal punishments, and to be punished by tears in hell. I will suffer then to be the object of the raillery of many, if my discourse may be fruitful to a few." In fact, the pastor should not be disheartened at seeing the little fruit produced by his exhortations. For example, although the Jewish people resisted the voice of the prophets, God did not cease to say to Isaiah, "Shout without ceasing, make your voice resound as a trumpet, announce to my people the crimes they have committed." (Isa. lviii.) St. Paul said to his disciple Timothy, "Press men in season and out of season; reprehend, supplicate, threaten, without ever growing weary in condemning their faults and instructing themselves." (Tim. xi. 4.) That is to say, without being weary at suffering their defects with a Christian sweetness, which comes from the charity you have for them, and for your great desire for their salvation, without becoming weary at combating their ignorance, their obstinacy, and conquering by the force of truth which you preach to them. "The more the wickedness of men increases, the more it must be combated, and the oftener and more strenuously should pastors preach," says St. Gregory. "Our Savior gives an example of this to us, when, after the Jews, resisting his doctrine, had said he was possessed by the devil, he instructed them more than ever, saying to the Jews, who had just outraged him so much, 'Verily, verily I say unto you, if anyone observes my word, he shall never die.'"

Pastors should never cease to speak against blasphemies, cursing, drunkenness, immodesty, injustice, and other disorders, although they should not flatter themselves with being able to destroy them entirely. Is anyone dispensed from preaching because few sinners have been converted by the best sermons?

It should be remembered that the number of those who resist the truth is always far greater than the number of those who yield to it; and also what a great gain is a soul ransomed by the blood of Christ, should it have been lost through sin, when by your efforts it has again been restored to God's friendship; should it not be deemed a sufficient recompense for your trouble?

It should nevertheless be hoped that, with the help of God, a greater number, enlightened by the light of God's truth, will be converted. The true way to gain souls to God is not to violate the rules of religion, but to observe them faithfully. In the small number of conversions made at the present day, we can see that it is usually the priests most zealous in attending to the rules of religion who effect them. If they have the grief of seeing some to whom the discipline of the gospel is too burdensome, and who wish to walk on the broad road, God gives them the consolation of seeing others repent of their opposition, yield to the force of truth, and thank them because they have not allowed them an indulgence which would be finally fatal.

The pastor ought to fear to destroy souls by a criminal complaisance, rather than by a rigorous severity; for those who prefer such dangerous pleasures to the sacraments are not worthy to receive them; if they approach the sacraments with this disposition, it can be only through unworthy motives, or as a mere form, like other duties, and for their damnation. It is an evil, it is true, to avoid the sacraments through attachment to pleasure, but a far greater evil to profane them. Whoever prefers to deprive himself of the sacraments rather than give up his pleasures, or yield to the wise advice of his pastor, excommunicates himself, and we can justly apply to him that expression of the prophet Osee, "Your ruin, O Israel, comes only from yourself."

The pastor ought to know that God wants the work, not the fruit of his work. He is guilty in remaining silent when he should speak; but he is not guilty when he speaks to the dead. He is obliged to plant and water the seed; he does not know if his work will succeed, because it is God who gives increase to what he sows; but if he does not sow, can he expect to reap?

He ought therefore to speak often against dances, to exhort with charity and mildness those who love dancing to renounce it; to ask of God, by frequent and fervent prayers, to open their hardened hearts to his exhortations; and if he is unable, with all his efforts and zeal, to suppress an evil of which he perceives the fatal consequences, he ought not to be discouraged still, but redouble in secret his prayers and groans, hoping that they will not be without fruit for some of those who are the objects of his prayers, or if they do not serve others, they will draw down on himself the grace of God, and insure his salvation.

16

PRECAUTIONS WITH WHICH A PASTOR OUGHT TO SPEAK AGAINST DANCING

In saying that it is necessary to speak against dancing, we do not mean to insinuate by that, that it is always expedient to devote long and frequent discourses in the pulpit to this delicate matter. This means, in an age so corrupt as ours, is not always the best, nor the most prudent. It may produce good effect in parishes where the pastors still find some attachment to religion, some docility to their advice, and respect for their persons, where the minds of the youth have not been entirely spoiled, nor their hearts corrupted; but in parishes where the faith is becoming extinct, where Jesus Christ is despised and persecuted in the person of his ministers, where the youth, imbued with the poison of bad doctrines, seek only the occasion to shake off the salutary yoke of religion, in order to deliver themselves with security and without reserve to all their ruling passions,—this means, far from producing the happy results anticipated, irritates and withdraws their minds, compromises the clergyman, and puts him out of a condition for doing good.

There are other means which a pastor can use without rendering himself hateful, and compromising his ministry.

When he has the grief to see that this abuse, so perni-cious to morals is engrafted strongly, and powerfully protected in his parish, he should undoubtedly labor to destroy it; he would fail in his duty if he did not; but to labor in it with success, he should proceed with a wise slowness, for experience proves that too much precipitation aggra-vates the evil, and often renders it incurable.

He should not speak of the disorder in the pulpit but when occasion offers, and as if incidentally; for to make it often the principal subject of his instructions is sometimes the means of augmenting and perpetuating it.

He ought, in the confessional, to forbid those most apt to listen to him to frequent the dance; he ought to refuse abso-lution to those for whom it is a proximate occasion of sin.

As to others, he ought to turn them from it by motives most apt to make impression on their minds; to show them the many dangers almost inseparable from it; to say to them with St. John Chrysostom, that the devil being called into the dance by the immodest airs, by the dissolute words and gaudy dress that accompany them, renders dancing apt to corrupt and seduce those who go to it; to remind them that they have renounced all these pomps and vanities in baptism, when, for the first time, they were admitted into communion with the church, and that they cannot partici-pate in these sinful pleasures without breaking the solemn covenant which they have sworn in the face of heaven and earth.

In fine, a pastor should study the spirit of his flock; the knowledge he will acquire will help and direct him in the choice of the most fit means to employ, for those that succeed in one parish fail in another, where the spirit of the people is different.

17

PARENTS OUGHT TO HINDER THEIR CHILDREN FROM GOING TO DANCES

Parents, in the bosom of their family, hold the place of God towards their children. They have not brought them into the world to make them reprobates, but to render them worthy of heaven; they should, therefore, keep them away from all amusements that tend to destroy them. Now, since reason and religion second us in saying that it is almost impossible to go to the dance without offending God, and experience teaches that many sins are committed at it, it follows clearly that parents ought to neglect nothing in order to make their children avoid it, and they will be very guilty before God if they do not.

Furthermore, the Holy Ghost orders parents especially to preserve with care the purity of their daughters, to redouble their vigilance over those who love to see and to be seen, who do not avoid the sight of men, and who have impudence in their eyes, for fear that they may ruin themselves if they find occasion for so doing. "Guard carefully a maiden inclined to licentiousness," he says to parents, "for fear" that, by committing some fault in her paternal house, "she may expose you to the insults of your enemies, that she may render you the object of the slander of a whole city, and the talk of the people, and that she may dishonor you before the whole world." (Eccles. xxvi. and xlii.)

From this it is easy to see how guilty a mother is who conducts her daughter to a dance, or who permits her to go thither alone, and spend there a part of the night. We may say with St. John Chrysostom, that she imitates the infamous Herodias, who made her daughter dance before Herod, in order to seduce him, and have an occasion of demanding from him the death of the greatest and holiest of men. Foolish mother, do you not see that you give occasion for saying of you and your daughter what St. Ambrose said of Herodias and her daughter? An adulterous woman like Herodias, said this holy doctor, could not teach her unfortunate daughter otherwise than to expose herself so immodestly in the dance. Can there be any shame in those who deliver themselves up to an exercise which is so contrary to modesty?

You do not see, then, that this girl who dances, imitates the gestures and indecent postures of comedians, and casts the poison of crime into the hearts of a great number of those who see her, by her movements and effeminate airs, and that she is the occasion of a crowd of sins! Who knows but those young men whose passions she has increased by the softness of her looks and behavior, may give themselves up to the greatest excesses? Is it strange, then, that we should see so many of these men dispute, quarrel, fight duels, and kill themselves for a fickle and imprudent woman, whom they have seen at the dance? Is there a city, is there even a village, which does not annually mourn at the account of these frightful crimes being renewed? Who can say but that your daughter may be the victim of your pliant and excessive complaisance, as young Dina was of her indiscreet curiosity, and as so many others are every day victims of the imprudence and blindness of their parents? Who knows, either, but that this maiden, on whom the Holy Ghost tells you "to redouble your watchfulness, when she loves to see and to be seen," and whom he orders you even "to guard strictly," when you see her inclined to sin, may be dishonored, against her will even, by those whose passions her imprudent attentions have inflamed, and for whom she will become, without knowing it herself, the occasion of innumerable sins? What happened at Cabries, near Aix, in Provence, is most fit to show you to what you expose your daughter every time that you have the weakness to conduct or allow her to go to dances. "It was the feast of this village; many of the young people of the environs had come to it. A peasant brought his daughter, hardly sixteen years old, to all the dances which were held in this place. The beauty of this young person excited the desires of fifteen half-intoxicated young men, who, after the festival, when they thought all at Cabries were asleep, hastened to the house in which she dwelt, broke open the doors, seized the unhappy father, whom they wounded severely, bound and gagged him, seized the young woman, whom they dragged into the neighboring woods, where many more of their companions were waiting. There this young victim was delivered to the brutality of thirty of these demons, who, after satisfying their criminal passions, maltreated her horribly."

What would be your bitter regrets, what your profound grief, if, by your imprudence, the chastity and innocence of your daughter were dashed against such a rock! Her dishonor would recoil on you; her bad conduct "would expose you," as the Holy Spirit says, "to the insults of your enemies, would render you the object of the censure of a whole city, and the laughing stock of the people, and would dishonor you before the whole world." Nevertheless, this is the evil to which you expose yourself when you permit her to go alone to these fatal places. You say that your daughter is too wise to think of sin; who has told you that she has not thought of it sometimes? Notwithstanding this apparent wisdom, which renders you confident on her account, she is perhaps interiorly devoured by an impure fire. She appears without reproach in your eyes, but if God gave you power to look into her soul, as he beholds it, you would perhaps be frightened at the multitude of sins which sully it. You think that she is wise; you do not then wish her to be so long; you are sorry that she has not yet lost her wisdom! Can we say that you wish her to preserve it, since you allow her to be exposed to dangers that may destroy it? Do you think that she can remain long chaste amidst young men who employ, in order to ruin her, all kinds of seduction, while the violence of their passions and the darkness of the night favor them in effecting their wicked designs? While you sleep tranquilly, the devil watches near her; he sets snares for her wavering virtue, which will be unable always to escape them, and he scatters in her road everything most likely to entrap her virtue. If she resists the first attack, she will succumb to the second. When she has made the first step in crime, she will advance in it more and more, daily. Your tears, your threats, the fear of dishonor, the wrath of heaven, will no longer correct her; the impure spirit which will rule her, blind and harden her heart, will hinder her from returning to God, and even from thinking of him. You glorify yourself when you see your daughter dance with grace and address, and when you hear people say that she is distinguished by this dangerous talent and in this fatal art; and you do not blush that you have left her unimbued even with the first principles of religion! You do not disturb yourself about whether your daughter offers her prayers mornings and evenings to God; you do not care whether she approaches the sacraments, or if she is assiduous in the divine service. Barbarous mother! Have you given her birth now only to make her be ruined tomorrow? Had it not been better that you had smothered her in the cradle than that you should bring her to life for the purpose of procuring for her, or allowing her to enjoy, such fatal pleasures? You would have deprived her only of the life of the body; but by your guilty complaisance you strip her of the life of grace, you kill her soul, and render her the instrument of her own eternal reprobation. "If anyone", says St. Paul, "has not care of his own, and particularly of those of his house, he has not the faith, he is worse than an infidel." (Tim. i. 5.) You not only neglect the education of your child, but even you teach her the art of corrupting herself, and you immolate her, in a manner, to the demon of impurity. You renounce not only the faith which orders you to bring up your daughter in the practice of all virtue, and to inspire her with a dread of everything evil, but you violate still further the laws of nature and the most divine rights and commands by allowing or procuring her pleasures which destroy the love of God, and give her a taste for what is most frivolous and criminal. If God does not punish you in this world, it is because he will punish you more rigorously in the next. The silence that he observes with regard to you is the silence of justice, which, serving only to harden you in sin, renders you more worthy of eternal punishment. You may find favor with him, perhaps, for your personal sins, but you will be condemned for those which you have allowed your daughter to commit. It is useless to observe that parents are not less obliged to forbid dancing to sons than to daughters. The following example comes to the support of this truth.

"A young man named Maurice was tenderly loved by his father, because he fulfilled faithfully all his duties. He took his recreations only with the family, or with virtuous companions, with the consent of his father and mother. His father said to him one day that he would allow him to go and amuse himself at a neighbor's, where there was a ball. 'My dear father,' he replied, 'I have no greater recreation than your company.' 'Well, my son,' said the father, 'we will go together.' The father conducted him a second and a third time to this sort of company. Maurice took pleasure in it, and began to forget his duties. He became attached to a woman who was not virtuous. The father perceived it, and forbade him to see her. But inclination, ruling the respect Maurice had for his father, led him to her every evening. The intrigue of Maurice with this woman became public, and created much rumor; the father received the reproach of it from his neighbors. 'Now then, my husband,' said his wife to him, 'you see the fruit of your complacency to your son. I have always been opposed to what goes on in these sorts of companies; I am guiltless of his crime before God; it is your fault.' 'I have been wrong,' answered the father; 'I should have followed your advice; it is through my error that my son has become a libertine; I must now correct him.' He called Maurice to him, and forbade him again to frequent this pernicious society. The son replied boldly that he was committing no sin, that he would continue to see her, and that he had no longer need of his advice in the matter. The father, who did not expect such an insolent answer, chastised on the spot his rebellious son. Hardly had Maurice received the correction than he enlisted in the cavalry. Some months afterwards he finished his life by a tragic death, having been bruised and killed under the feet of his horse." Young men, reflect on this example. Maurice is virtuous as long as he avoids dancing; but as soon as he frequents it, he ruins and corrupts himself. Fathers and mothers, the more your children are inclined to go to dances, the more dangerous they are for them, and the more you should keep them away. Fear lest your negligence may draw down on you and them, on this account, the severest chastisements of God.

MASTERS AND MISTRESSES SHOULD HINDER THEIR SERVANTS FROM GOING TO DANCES

"If anyone," says St. Paul, "has not care of his own, and particularly of those of his own house, he is worse than an infidel, and has renounced the faith." St. Paul puts no distinction here between children and servants; he makes masters and mistresses see that they should watch over the conduct of their servants as they would over their own children, incline them to virtue by their conversation and example, and use the authority they have over them in order to make them avoid sin and its occasions; they ought, then, to forbid them dances where they run very great danger, being for the most part orphans, or removed from their parents. Reason and religion second us in saying that masters and mistresses will have to account before God for their servants as well as children.

DANCES DO NOT GIVE A YOUNG WOMAN A CHANCE TO GET MARRIED SOONER, OR MORE ADVANTAGEOUSLY

Woe to those fathers and mothers who are more zealous for making their children well to do in the world, than holy and pious; who, far from watching carefully over their purity, do not fear to expose them to the danger of losing it in these contagious assemblies, where everything seen and heard, everything done, excites bad thoughts, criminal desires, and impure sensations, which degrade the imagination and sully the heart! Even though these fathers and mothers should occasion that their children be better established in the world, what good would it be, since these advantageous marriages will have been effected by losing the fear of God? They would serve only to render them more vicious, and to bring them more easily to hell. "What doth it profit a man," says the Savior, "if he gain the whole world, and lose his soul?" Wretched are those children who have such blind and infidel parents! It would be better for them never to have been born, than to be so of parents who seem to have given them a body that they might be able to kill the soul by neglecting to watch over their behavior.

But parents and children are in great error, believing

that by going to dances wealthy acquaintances will be formed, and marriages more readily accomplished. If a young woman be mild, modest, diligent, obedient to her parents, regular in her conduct, the fame of her virtues will draw her from oblivion, and make her known enough; she will obtain the respect and esteem of honest men, who will never speak of her but with praise. Even the worldly, in whose eyes she has no other fault than that of not participating in their foolish pleasures, cannot but feel a sentiment of respect and esteem for her, on account of her virtues. If a young man who prefers libertinism to virtue, does not seek her acquaintance, ought she to be afflicted thereat? Ought she not, on the contrary, to be glad that she shall not have as husband a young man who probably would render her unhappy, and whose perverted example and wicked discourse would end perhaps in perverting herself? Is it not a happiness that a libertine of this sort avoids her, and leaves her in peace in her father's house?

But if he is a good man and well instructed, who prefers virtue to vice, he will be happy to obtain for a wife such a virtuous young woman. They will be, as the Holy Ghost says, "the recompense of each other's merits"—"*Mulier bona debitur viro pro factis* suis," (Prov. xxix.) If the fear of offending God hinders this maiden from appearing at these profane assemblies, her good Father in heaven, who is never conquered in generosity, will not permit such a praise-worthy motive to be an obstacle to her happiness. "Seek first the kingdom of heaven, and all else shall be added over and above." In fact, if God takes care of a poor sparrow, if he wishes not a single hair of our head to fall without his permission, can he remain indifferent in regard to a young woman who, in order to serve him, avoids these profane dances? What can he refuse this beloved child, who is entirely devoted to him, and who, by her faithful discharge of her duties, renders herself worthy of his love? He will send her from afar, as he did to Sarah, a Tobias who will render her happy.

You, young woman, who, in order to be sought in marriage, do not omit any opportunity to appear at dances, who appear so giddy, so free in your manner, and who permit all sorts of liberties from young men, do not think that this is the way by which you will best succeed. Are you then so little acquainted with the world as not to see that this young man, who takes these liberties, would be very sorry to have you for a wife? He wishes to divert himself and pass his time with you; but the thought never once enters his head of uniting his lot to yours. You may be certain that when he is in other societies he does not spare your reputation, and that you often become the object of his jokes: he does not fail to tell others the conversations which you have had with him; he makes no scruple of publishing everything most secret which has passed between you. Do you think that any man of good sense would prefer a flirting, giddy woman, a dancer by profession, to a young woman of sober, modest, and decent disposition, who leads a Christian life in retirement? Undoubtedly he will take pleasure in dancing with you, but at heart he will not esteem you—he will despise you; he will regard you as a woman without restraint, and of very equivocal virtue. He will easily imagine that you are not more modest with others than with himself, and that you would be far more foolish than now if you were once engaged in the bonds of marriage.

Thus you see that young women who are wise and modest, and who fly every sort of dangerous reunion, are more honored and sought after than those of the opposite dispositions, and that they find more virtuous husbands, and form more happy marriages, than dancers.

When young persons are prepared for marriage, by the practice of virtue, by avoiding sin and all that leads to it, they receive, with the nuptial benediction, all the favors of the God of Abraham, of Isaac, and of Jacob. These fortunate husbands, special objects of heaven's favor, spend their days full of happiness. If adversity causes them to suffer, they have, in their submission to heaven's decrees, the consoling hope, that *the passing pain which they suffer on earth,* and of which they make good use, will procure for them *an immense quality of glory in heaven.*

AFTERWORD

It is easy to see that the dance is a pomp of the devil, a snare of the impure spirit, an artifice of hell to seduce men, a fire which burns the hearts of youth, which excites in them all sorts of immodest passions, and exposes them to the extreme danger of being ruined.

The Holy Fathers are then right in saying that, *if one goes chaste to the dance, he returns from it impure, and that the soul receives there many wounds, although the body receives no injury.* They were so far from allowing young persons to go to dances, that they thought even the virtues and austerities of an anchorite were not a sufficient safeguard against the dangers to be met with at them.

In effect, if young persons could go to dances without seeing the disorders that reign in them, without hearing the obscene discourses which are held in them; if they had suffi-cient strength of mind to be attentive to nothing but God; if they could go to them without disobeying their lawful supe-riors, and without giving bad example to their neighbor,—I agree that they could do so without offending God: but since young people appear there only with the pomp and finery of the most seductive luxury, and they pay great attention to these accompaniments, in order to be more attractive; as young men go to these dances only to feed their eyes on the beauty, elegance, and suppleness of young women, and their ears with the effeminate sound of voluptuous music; since both are ruled by the most violent passions, and since the excitement of the dance renders them still more violent; since young men frequent them only to corrupt and be corrupted, by keeping up libertine conversations, by immodest looks and indecent gestures, and even, when they can, and as they can often and dare almost always, by some criminal liberties; since they cannot go to these places without bringing many others who commit there also many faults, and without disobeying the church and the gospel, which, in order the more efficaciously to turn them from these amusements, display all the dangers to be encountered in dances to them; since they are occupied there in doing evil and finding out means to commit sin, rather than to please God,—would it not be an impiety to say, that they can go there without offending God, without incurring his indignation, and without rendering themselves worthy of the punishments of eternity?

Though, by reasoning, one can find that certain dances are innocent, it is not less true, by a consequence of the corruption natural to man, that they are almost always an occasion of temptation and of fall for many, and particularly for young men and women. Does not this reason suffice to cause us to abolish absolutely such a fruitful source of sin? What matters it that you can absolutely dance without sin, if almost always sin is committed by so doing, either after having danced, or if, not committing sin in so doing, one exposes himself visibly to the danger of sinning?

Sin is so great an evil that one cannot put too great a

distance between himself and it. To go precisely to the boundary line, so to speak, which separates virtue from vice, is risking too much the danger of falling into sin which you seem to avoid. "Abstain from every thing like evil," said St. Paul to the Thessalonians. We cannot be too careful when eternity is at stake, says Tertullian—*"Nula satis magna securitas, ubi periclitatur aeternitas."*

But, even though you should not fall into the sins which dancing exposes its votaries to, you would not be innocent on that account in going to it; for he who exposes himself voluntarily to the danger of committing a mortal sin, contracts the malice of the sin to which he exposes himself, even though sin should not follow. The commandment which forbids a sin forbids equally to expose one's self to the danger of committing it. It is in this sense that the Holy Ghost teaches us that he who loves danger will perish in it —*"qui amat periculum, in eo peribit." (Eccles.* iii. 27.)

Jesus Christ orders us to renounce an employment, an estate, or a society, which would expose us to the danger of being lost; he orders us also to renounce, therefore, dances, since they give birth ordinarily to pride, vanity, impurity, rivalry, jealousy, quarrels, murdering, hatred; and to many other vices which prevent their votaries from entering heaven. Jesus Christ orders us to repress the levity of our mind; to mortify our senses; to be on our guard against the weakness of our flesh, against the force of our passions, against the malice and cunning of the tempter; to avoid the least occasions of being tempted; to be moderate in our pleasures, and to resist the perversity of the maxims and joys of the world. He forbids, therefore, dances also, since they offer us all these dangers, without any means of preserving ourselves from their contagious influence.

20

IMPORTANT ADVICE TO A
YOUNG MAN

If you wish to please the Lord, young man, you should obey his will, and be submissive to him. You will certainly disobey him if you persist in going to dances and balls; for he forbids you to be in the company *of her that is a dancer;* he reminds you, at the same time, that her charms are not without danger for your innocence. You are young, and your youth is a powerful reason why you should submit to the command of God; when one is young, he is more weak and fragile; one falls more easily, and recovers himself with more difficulty. God furthermore says to you that *if you love danger, you will perish in it,* if you go habitually to these worldly assemblies, where all is danger, can we not say with reason that you love danger, that you seek it, and that you will not escape perishing in it? Is it not enough for you to have to combat a multitude of involuntary temptations, which all the objects that surround you create; to have to struggle against enemies which you meet at every step; to have to resist continually your passions, without going to cast your-self blindly into snares that you can easily avoid, and into which many others, stronger and more virtuous than you, have fallen? How many have there not been who have found the ruin of their innocence in balls and in dances, and who will groan for eternity beneath the fatal consequences of the madness that urged them to these perfidious pleasures in this life!

You pretend that you never commit any sin at dances, and that you come forth from these circles of lubricity with your soul as pure as when you entered them. If you speak the truth, I no longer regard you as a man, but as an angel, who has no human frailty. If you are not tormented by any impure thought in these places, you are happier than St. Paul, that great apostle, who was obliged to reduce his body into subjection, in order to preserve the precious treasure of innocence that was in him; you are happier than those illustrious penitents, who, retired in the most frightful deserts, where they occupied themselves only with God, nevertheless were at great pains to repress the excitements of the flesh; you are more fortunate than St. Jerome, who, buried in the depth of solitude, where he delivered his body to the most painful mortification, where he had no companions but the beasts of the fields, nevertheless complained bitterly of the rude assaults which the demon of impurity made on him. Can I believe that you are more engrafted in virtue than these holy personages, and that you do not carry as well as they *the treasure of your innocence in a fragile vessel?* Can I believe that you can remain safe in places where an anchorite would be in danger?

You pretend that you commit no sin at them; but do you know what sin is, and what it is not, all that pleases God, and all that displeases him? Have you not good reason to fear that the excessive passion you have conceived for these pleasures may have covered your eyes with a thick cloud, to hinder you from seeing the dangers you run, and the sin you commit at them? If it is true that you have not yet sinned at them, I think you expose yourself to the danger of so doing. Who has assured you that you may go to dances like so many others, and that you will not perish in the danger which you have the folly to seek like them? The remembrance of David, whom a single glance led into sin, and of Solomon, whose lust perverted his heart and mind,—ought it not to make you tremble for yourself? Ah! I fear that you, who are but a feeble reed, which the least breath makes bend, will not be able to resist the storm which crashes to pieces the stoutest oaks.

Besides, why do you go with gayety of heart to be present at these assemblies, where you know for certain that there are always some who offend God? Through love and respect for him you should feel great grief at seeing him offended; you will show very little affection and attachment for him if you behold with an indifferent eye all these disorders which outrage him. A well-instructed son will not willingly go into a society where no one respects or esteems his father; a faithful subject will not be among a troop of conspirators who meditate the death of his king. Is not God your Father and King? Can you be allowed to be present without necessity in the society of sinners who are his enemies? Can you willingly take part in their criminal joys without afflicting the heart of this good Father? Ought you not to fear that, by frequenting them, the perversity of their discourse and example may make pernicious impressions on you, and induce you to shake off the yoke of virtue and religion? Does it not ordinarily happen that we become like those whose company we keep? You know that you are on earth only to work out your salvation and merit heaven; but to enter heaven you must be holy, you must be pure; for it is written that nothing impure will enter it; and to be holy, do not think that it suffices to respect the life of your neighbor, his honor and well being, to abstain from those crimes that lead men to the scaffold; you must also defend your heart from the impressions of pleasure, avoid too free looks, impure desires, obscene words, equivocal pleasantries, capable of two significations; you should thus avoid those dangers presented in dances, where there are means of saving yourself from them; for temerity does not hinder from falling into danger, but leads naturally to it. If you be not holy, it is certain you will be repulsed; for you cannot possibly reach heaven by the road to hell. You cannot believe that people arrive at the sojourn of the blessed by the way of pleasures and amusements as well as by the way of sufferings and mortifications.

If you should read in the lives of the saints that some of them frequented balls and shows without difficulty, that they did not distinguish themselves from the rest of men, and that they conformed to all the customs of the world, you would find your ideas revolt in reading details of this kind, and you would conceive, against your will, strong doubts on the feigned virtues of these persons; their sanctity would appear to you very strange and imperfect. Can you then with consistency approve in yourself what you condemn in others? What you confess to be a sin for saints cannot possibly help your salvation. If you wish decidedly to save yourself, follow in the footsteps of those who have succeeded in the important affair of their salvation. If you are too weak, by your avowal, to do all the good that they have done, avoid at least all the evil which they have avoided.

You would not wish that death would surprise you in a ball. If a prophet came to tell you, on the part of God, that you would die in a month, you would be careful to go there no more; you would think it more prudent to dispose your-self to appear before the Judge of all men, and endeavor to render yourself favorable to him. But who has told you that you have another month to live? Jesus Christ, on the contrary, forewarns you to be always ready, and that he will come at an hour you know not. It will perhaps be today, perhaps tomorrow, perhaps this night, that he will demand your soul. He has called happy him who watched so that he was ready, when the Lord came, to open the gate when he knocked. Suppose yourself at the last moment of your life, as some time or other you will incontestably be; what line of conduct would you wish to have held in this moment which will decide your eternal happiness or your eternal misery? Will the remembrance of balls and other dangerous plea-sures be then consoling to you? Would you not wish then to have constantly practiced virtue, to have always avoided the least occasions of sin, and to have expiated by the tears of a sincere penitence the faults which you have had the misfor-tune to commit? Why, then, are you so base as to follow the torrent of the customs of a corrupt world? The saints have expressed only contempt and hatred for these silly joys and worldly pleasures. They now are happy in heaven; eternal happiness is the recompense for earthly mortification. Will you be so foolish and blind as to think that you can, without displeasing God and losing your salvation, stray from the straight road where they lie, and that you can transgress with impunity the rules of prudence, that you ought scrupu-lously to observe?

The saints thought that when there was a question involving eternity, there could never be too great security. And you, can you be tranquil and unsolicitous about your salvation in the midst of the dangerous occasions of the world, by opening your heart to the most dangerous emotions, by allowing your soul to wander through so many objects capable of seducing it, by satisfying your eyes on everything that vanity can display, and lending an attentive ear to the language of pleasure? You wish to partake of the happiness of the saints, and you will not do violence to yourself, like them, in order to gain heaven! Do then to save your soul what you would do to save the life of your body. If, when you were on the point of making a journey, someone came to tell you that the road you were to take was full of danger, that the robbers had massacred many travelers on it, and that you ran the risk of falling into their hands, you would not certainly follow such a dangerous route, however short and commodious it might be in other respects. You would take another, no matter how long or difficult. You are told that you run great danger for your soul in balls and dances; if you have a real wish to be saved, you will shun these places, so full of disorders and foolish pleasures. You will not follow the crowd of those who go to bend the knee to Baal, but the small number of those who go to adore the Savior in his temple, who work without ceasing to obtain their salvation, and try to enter by the narrow gate which leads to heaven. If you are truly zealous for your salvation, you will be careful to follow in the traces of those who gained heaven; you will not follow the footsteps of those young fools who take the broad road to hell, but you will conform your conduct to the holy maxims of the gospel, and to the solemn promises which you have made in your baptism by renouncing Satan, all his works and all his pomps, the principal of which are plays, balls, and dances, and which you cannot violate without rendering yourself guilty of a species of perjury and apostasy, since it would be violating your oath, and abandoning Jesus Christ to follow Satan, whom you have solemnly renounced.

21

IMPORTANT ADVICE TO A YOUNG WOMAN

You, young woman, who are desirous of preserving your innocence, shun balls and dances, where you can hardly appear without losing your chastity. Even though you should not fall into those sins which brought a deluge on the earth, which brought fire from heaven on Sodom, and which, as St. Paul says, ought not to be named among Christians, you will, however, be guilty for having despised the will of God, by exposing yourself willingly to danger to perish in it. But can you reply that you will not fall into it, and that you have nothing to fear for your innocence "in a circle the centre of which is the devil, and his angels the circumference," says St. John Chrysostom; where those spirits of darkness employ a multitude of young men without religion and without morals to seize your heart? Can you reply that you will not fall into the power of the devil, as the woman of whom Tertullian speaks, who, being present at dances and public spectacles where the Christians never went then, was suddenly possessed by a furious demon? The priests who came to her help asked the devil why he had dared to seize a Christian woman. "I had leave," answered the demon, "*because she went into a place of my domain.*"

Behold, young woman, to what you expose yourself every time you go to dances. You renounce, in some sort, Jesus Christ to submit yourself to the authority of the devil. If he does not exercise his fury on your body, as on her whom Tertullian mentions, he exercises it on your soul, in making you lose love of piety, the fear of God, in rendering it indifferent to its salvation, in inclining it more to sin, and stripping it of the life of grace.

You think, perhaps, that dances cannot hurt you, because you have been educated in the practice of Christian virtues, because you love virtue and fear evil, and because you are disposed to resist all the attacks of the tempter, and repress all the irregular motions of concupiscence; you are in error: all that you see at balls, all that you hear at them, all that you feel, will soon make you lose sight of the good resolutions you have taken, and the religious principles that you have received; will substitute for your virtues the most dishonoring vices, and, instead of this beautiful modesty, that ornaments your looks and appearance, will make you adopt the impudence of those who know not how to blush. However strong in virtue you may be, a fatal experience will teach you soon that it is as impossible for you to be in the bosom of corruption without being corrupted, as it is to be in the midst of flames and not be burned.

How many young women like you do we not see, who were pure, and always had a dread even of the shade of sin, returning from a ball with passions more lively and head-strong, with modesty weakened and incapable of sustaining their shock and arresting their ravages, with more frequent and dangerous temptations, with a more decided inclination for vice, and less love for virtue? And all this from getting attached to young men, who made them fine promises, not once thinking of keeping any one of them, and who, besides, were not fit for them! How many have we not seen enter these direful places with a calm, pure heart, and leave them with a deeply corrupted heart, and cruelly tormented by all the impure thoughts and remorse that the impure spirit creates! If, in order to escape the mortal enemy who devours them, they plunge more deeply into shameful disorders, far from finding peace in so doing, they experience the most painful torments. The Holy Ghost has said that there is no peace for the sinner—*Non est pax impiis.* Avoid, young woman, these pernicious diversions, which will, in an instant, take away your peace and innocence of heart, and which will soon make you experience that, if the commencements of sin appear sweet, the consequences of it are very bitter.

You think, also, perhaps, that you have nothing to fear from the dangers that the dance offers, because your intention is never to appear there without being accompanied by your parents. You are still in error; for however vigilant they may be, they cannot guard your looks, nor hinder them from falling on dangerous objects, which will seduce your heart; they cannot direct your thoughts, still less hinder you from having bad ones, and from being pleased with them, and consenting to them. How many times have parents to combat the foolish loves of a young daughter, who had been their consolation till she became known to a young man at some ball, where he won her heart in their presence, while, perhaps, they applauded themselves on their model of wisdom! An impure glance, a too free expression, which having fallen on her heart, like a spark on straw, may seduce her soul from God, and kindle therein an impure fire.

Behold, young woman, what will infallibly happen to

you, if you remain steadfast in going to dances: all that is in these places should serve only to alarm you, and you will find nothing in them to make you confident. The presence of your parents, the principles of a Christian education, and a long habit of virtue, will not guarantee your safety from the contagion with which these dances are infected. You will not be saved where so many other virtuous persons, perhaps more pious than you, have been shipwrecked. You will perish there, like them, because you have the same weakness and the same fragility; because you will encounter there the same dangers. Besides, you cannot go there without joining yourself to many libertine men and women, *who swallow iniquity like water,* without participating by your presence in all the disorders that they commit there, in the dissolute expressions, licentious conversations that they hold in them, and in all the criminal liberties that they permit. You cannot go there without loading yourself with a multitude of sins, which will not be less yours than if you committed them.

I will go further, and say, that you cannot go to dances without hurting your reputation; for if one sees you go to them often, you will be regarded, and justly, as a fickle maiden, thoughtless and giddy, and one cannot but doubt of the purity of your intentions, and the innocence of your morals. Can anyone believe that a young woman, who, every time she finds occasion, appears with effrontery in the midst of men, with a brazen look that seems to provoke them to impurity, with dress half covering the body, and conducting herself in the most foolish and indecent manner, can have pure morals, or much shame, for any length of time? Even some of the pagans, according to Æmilius Probus, thought that the dance should be ranked among vicious things—*"Scimus saltare etiam in vitiis poni."*

Cato accused Murena, a Roman consul, of having danced in Asia. Cicero, in his eloquent pleading in favor of the latter, took care not to justify him if he had danced, but he firmly denied the fact. What he said in this respect is remarkable. "If Murena has danced, O Cato," exclaimed this great orator, "the accusation you bring against him is strong and grave; but if he has not danced, it is an extreme outrage you do him. To render credible what you advance against him, you should consider first and show us to what vices he whom you accuse must have been subject; *for no one sober is ever found to dance, unless he be a fool.*"

"Blush!" exclaims hereupon Cardinal Bellarmine; "a pagan has thought more sanely than you, and a pagan one day will condemn you on the judgment day: mere natural knowledge put this pagan in a condition to teach us that dancing is only fit for drunkards and fools. And you who are children of God, and enlightened by the celestial knowledge of the gospel,—you, among whom such absurdities ought not even to be mentioned,—you have the folly to deliver yourselves to dances, even on the most solemn and sacred days!"

Such is the idea pagans had of dancers of both sexes— an idea which shows you that you cannot go to dances and balls without opening your heart to the shameful allurements of vice, without destroying your modesty, shame, and the other virtues which make the ornaments of your sex, and without compromising your reputation, which, next to your salvation, is the most precious possession you have on earth.

If the pagans, aided by reason alone, saw so many indecencies and disorders in balls, what would they not have seen if they had been, as you, instructed by the burning, bright lights of faith? They would have seen what is really in them, and what the angels see in them; they would have seen a horrible massacre of souls killing each other, women whom the devil possesses, who wound mortally miserable men, and men who pierce the hearts of women by their criminal idolatry; they would have seen there a crowd of demons who enter the souls by all the senses of the body, who poison them by every object they see, who lead their dupes by a thousand chains, who prepare for them a thousand punishments, who trample them under their feet and laugh at their illusion and blindness; they would have seen a God who beholds these souls with wrath, and who abandons them to the fury of the devils. Behold, young woman, what you yourself will see there, if you are careful to attend to your faith, and use its celestial torch to drive away the thick darkness with which the passions of your heart and the false maxims of the world have covered your mind. Do not judge dancing by what the world thinks and says of it; it is so connected with crime, that more sin is not seen committed in the most criminal amusements; but judge it by what your faith says of it, silence your passions that you may hear the language she holds on it, listen to the salutary advice she gives you, and you will have a horror of those diversions which you now love with a sort of madness.

Follow not the maxims of the world; these maxims would kill your soul by stripping it of the life of grace, and rendering it worthy of the flames of hell. Follow the maxims of Jesus Christ, you will live in his spirit, and you will merit to live one day with him in his glory. The world wishes you to lead on this earth an agreeable and pleasing life; but such a life leads to eternal misery. Jesus Christ wishes you to lead a penitent and mortified life, and such a life leads to the enjoyment of the immutable pleasures of heaven.

See what happened to the wicked rich man, who was

clothed in purple and fine linen, who made good cheer every day, and who was hurled into the flames of hell, where he suffers cruelly still—"*Crucior in hac flamma;*" whilst the poor Lazarus, who died of hunger at Dives' gate, is in the bosom of Abraham, where he enjoys perfect happiness.

Do not allow yourself to be led by the example of others, but mourn scandal, the more it is extended. Deplore their blindness, which hinders them from seeing the evil they do, and the crimes of which they are the deplorable cause. If a wish to go to dances seizes you, call to mind that they are a remnant of paganism, contrary to the gospel, a school of prostitution, a resort of iniquity, where people go with pride, where no one can stay with any modesty, whence people go forth with impure thoughts and desires, where the excitement and variety of the objects, the freedom of expressions and manners, will embolden you to commit without shame what you would blush at now.

Recollect that Sodom was reduced to ashes for being abandoned to the infamous pleasures of impurity; that the children of Israel were chastised by the most terrible scourges for having danced indecently and with idolatry around the golden calf; that the impious Herod murdered the greatest and most holy of the children of men, lost his crown and possessions, and died in extreme misery, for having imprudently opened his heart to the charms of a dancer; that Dina, daughter of Jacob and sister of the twelve patriarchs, was seized and dishonored in a public *fête,* an injury which was resented by her brothers at the expense of a whole town, the inhabitants of which they slaughtered most horribly.

Recollect that the pleasure sought in dances is nothing else than a mortal poison concealed under a false sweetness, which may appear agreeable when one drinks it, but which makes us feel all its bitterness as soon as drank; and that, by a just punishment of God, the deeper we dip into pleasure and sin, the more unhappy we become. Remember, in fine, that God tells us that nothing impure will enter heaven, and only those of pure heart will have the happiness of seeing him—*"Beati mundo corde, quoniam ipsi Deum videbunt."*

If you feel inclined to go to a dance, be persuaded it is your concupiscence that wishes to satisfy itself, and that it is the devil who makes you hear his seductive voice, in order to make you fall into his snares. If anyone invites you to a dance, do not accept the perfidious invitation; repel with horror that hand that wishes to lead you to it—it is the hand of the devil.

Ah, could you say with the virtuous Sara, that *you never mingled with those who do nothing but enjoy themselves, and who conduct themselves with levity,* and that you never mingled in the society of those who do nothing but enjoy pleasures, who think only of dancing, and who, after a life of foolish pleasure, will be cast into hell!

Follow the advice of the Holy Ghost; avoid those places where sinners assemble, for fear of being implicated in their crimes; for if they render themselves worthy of death by doing what they do, you would be not less worthy of it than they, since you imitate them and approve of their deeds.